NEANDERTHAL MAN

Reconstruction drawing of Neanderthal man from R.E. Leakey and R. Lewin, *Origins*, London 1977. Robert Harding Picture Library.

Neanderthal Man

Myra Shackley

Archon Books

First published 1980 in England by
Gerald Duckworth & Co. Ltd.
and in the U.S.A. as an
Archon Book, an imprint of
The Shoe String Press, Inc.
995 Sherman Avenue
Hamden, Connecticut 06514

ISBN 0-208-01850-6

LC 80-65076

British Library Cataloguing in Publication Data
Shackley, Myra Lesley
  Neanderthal man.
  1. Mousterian culture
  2. Neanderthal race
  I. Title
  573'.3   GN772.2.M6

Photoset by
Specialised Offset Services Limited, Liverpool
and printed in Great Britain by
Unwin Brothers Limited, Old Woking

Contents

Preface

Homo sapiens neanderthalensis (Neanderthal man) is the name given to a group of different varieties of our own species *Homo sapiens sapiens* which evolved around 90,000 BC, developing a complex material culture far more advanced than anything before. Unfortunately the discovery of the first Neanderthal remains occurred when the climate of thought was unfavourable to accepting a 'primitive' looking creature as in some way connected with our own evolution. The fight for the establishment of at least some variants of Neanderthal as potential ancestors has been a long one, and it is only just being realised that what used to be considered as a simple evolutionary side-branch, becoming extinct around 35,000 BC due to the evolution of superior modern-type man, is in reality more intricate. 'Neanderthal man' is a general term used for a group of people of diverse physical type, although it was at first applied to the more extreme forms whose appearance was very different from our own. However, the Neanderthals were responsible for immense advances in cultural evolution, setting the scene for the behavioural traits that used to be thought peculiar to our own species. We know that some forms of Neanderthal became extinct, but it is possible that others evolved into *Homo sapiens sapiens*. Certainly modern man and different Neanderthals co-existed for quite a long period, often in the same areas. The tool assemblages generally associated with Neanderthal man are called 'Mousterian', and a number of well-defined stone-working traditions exist. But it would seem that not all Neanderthals made tools of Mousterian type, since some Mousterian assemblages were made by modern-looking man and the simple equation of

Neanderthal=Mousterian has now been discarded.

This book does not purport to be a systematic survey of all the sites and skeletal remains of Neanderthal man, a subject so vast and so controversial that it would be better treated in a series of monographs with contributions from disciplines ranging from palaeontology to phonetics. The theme discussed here is a simple one. It is suggested that throughout the history of mankind there seem to have been certain horizons which mark such great cultural steps forward that they have in the past been referred to as 'revolutions'. This term has now gone out of favour with archaeologist and historian alike, and it is fashionable to view events as a slow and logical progression rather than a series of rapid 'bursts'. It is, however, indisputable that at certain slices across time events progressed with great rapidity, the correspondingly great cultural changes being evidenced in the archaeological record. Perhaps the first of these watersheds occurred as early as five or six million years ago, when the earliest ancestors of man stopped being eaten and became predators, an event probably accompanied by the 'invention' of tool-using and, later, tool-making. Tools compensated for the lack of sharp teeth or the ability to run fast, and allowed our ancestors to survive and prosper in a potentially hostile world. But for several million years afterwards it seems that man, or proto-man, did not progress beyond the group organisation level shared by most primates, save in the evolution of language, and the benefits (inter-tribal communication, the development of oral traditions) which this brought. If we think of man as a primate with something which no other primate has, an uncertain 'something' which might be an extra sense or has even been called a 'soul', then we should be able to search the archaeological record for the first tangible evidence and determine at which level of our physical evolution *Homo sapiens* became truly human. Humanity may be manifested in different ways; care for the sick, the beginnings of a belief in an afterlife shown by careful burials with provisions for a journey, the beginning of art. All these traits appear in the archaeological record in association with the remains of Neanderthal man, at a cultural watershed beginning around 90,000 BP, and this book attempts to explore their evolution.

No apology is made for making a selection of sites and examples exemplifying this theory, as the book is a 'personal view' of Neanderthal. No doubt many will quarrel with the ideas expressed here and many will put forward sites where the evidence appears to be contradictory. But if this book dispels the lingering remnants of the conviction that Neanderthal man was a sub-human brute it will have served its purpose, and if the reader is tempted to follow the lines of enquiry suggested by the bibliography he will be qualified to agree or disagree for himself.

I am indebted to the following individuals for their assistance with various aspects of this book: Mary Allden, Mrs M.R. Ali, Desmond Collins, Rene Dahinden, Dennis Fowler, Dr V. Gabori-Csank, M. Jean Guichard, Professor R. Klein, Mrs C. Lewis, Professor J. Napier, Mrs A.E.S. Partington, Nick Pollard, Dr D.A. Roe, Derrick Rowles.

M.L.S.

Illustrations

1

Evolution and Neanderthal Man

'Neanderthal' man is a colloquial name used rather loosely to describe a group of hominids who bear a resemblance to the famous skeleton of *Homo sapiens neanderthalensis** found in a cave in the Neander valley near Dusseldorf, Germany (p.14). The term is used in practice to embrace a series of different forms, as the Neanderthals were not a 'race' as we understand it but rather a group of hominids branching out from the main family tree, another branch of which led to modern man (*Homo sapiens sapiens*). The first Neanderthal finds were made in Europe and it chanced that the skeletons discovered belonged to extreme and probably highly specialised Neanderthals, culminating in an evolutionary sideline. These extreme or 'classic' Neanderthals are quite different from less specialised populations found later in Europe and elsewhere. A series of intermediate forms is now known which seems to represent members of less specialised groups of man who existed *before* Neanderthal time, co-existed with Neanderthal and possibly survived him. It is possible that one of these less specialised forms led to modern man, or that *Homo sapiens sapiens* evolved from yet another branch of the family tree (Fig.1). The general picture evoked by the term 'Neanderthal' is of the most extreme variety, a relatively short, broad and stocky man with powerful limbs, who stood fully upright and whose postcranial skeleton is remarkable for the crudely

---

* The original spelling is Neander*th*al, not Neandertal. Vallois (1952) said that this should be retained for *Homo neanderthalensis* but changes in German orthography made the spelling Neander*t*al more correct. This has resulted in much division of opinion and a haphazard mixture of the two names. The original spelling has been retained in this book.

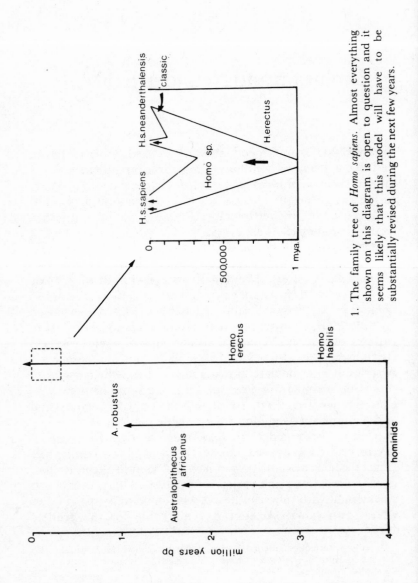

1. The family tree of *Homo sapiens*. Almost everything shown on this diagram is open to question and it seems likely that this model will have to be substantially revised during the next few years.

inscribed muscles and curvature of the limb bones (indicative of great strength). Early reconstructions were made (unfortunately) from the skeleton of an elderly Neanderthal from La Chapelle-aux-Saints (France, p.15) who had suffered from various diseases including acute arthritis. This misled anthropologists of the day into envisaging Neanderthal as a bent-kneed shuffling individual of sub-human appearance and mentality, which was simply not the case. Culturally Neanderthal man was the most advanced hominid species until the appearance of anatomically modern man, and it is with Neanderthal that we see the appearance of the distinctively 'human' traits nurtured and brought to fruition by our own species. The facial appearance of Neanderthal man was different from ours, as can be seen from a comparison of the skull profiles (Fig.2). The frontal region of the skull was flattened, the brow ridges more prominent than ours and the occipital region expanded into a bun-like swelling. Reasons for these anatomical peculiarities are discussed below (p.22). The strange skull shape resulted in a large face and broad nasal aperture, suggesting that he had a large flattened nose, a stout but chinless jaw and big teeth arranged in a horseshoe-shaped arcade. The molar teeth often have enlarged pulp cavities (taurodontism) an allegedly 'primitive' characteristic.[1]

We do not yet know the reason for the distinctive head shape and face type characteristic of Neanderthal man, although theories such as climatic adaptation have been advanced by a number of writers and functional specialisation by others.[2] The 'classic' Neanderthal head shape differed from all other Pleistocene* hominids except the middle eastern Neanderthals (p.121).

Vallois and Vandermeersch[3] have emphasised that we must dispense with the widely-held idea that the only maker of the Mousterian stone industry was Neanderthal man. Mousterian industries in some areas do not necessarily imply Neanderthal populations and blade tool industries of Upper Palaeolithic

---

* The geological period which encompasses the last Ice Age and lasted from *c*. 1.6 million years to 10,000 years BC.

type do not imply the presence of anatomically modern man. It is, however, true that no modern remains are definitively associated with a Mousterian stone industry, nor are there any Neanderthal remains with an Upper Palaeolithic* industry, although people and industries transitional between

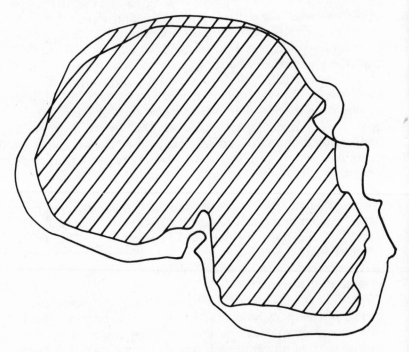

2.   Skull profiles of 'classic' and 'progressive' Neanderthals. The shaded area illustrates the modern appearance of the Skuhl 4 skull, in marked contrast to the heavy brow ridges, receding chin and sloping brow of the 'classic' skull from La Chapelle-aux-Saints (after Constable).

* The term 'Palaeolithic' means 'old stone age'. The Lower Palaeolithic stretches from the first appearance of tool making in Africa over 3 million years ago to the appearance of the Mousterian industries at 90,000-75,000 BP. These latter were made during the Middle Palaeolithic, which was succeeded by the Upper Palaeolithic, at about 35,000 BP, in which tools were made on stone blades, and their makers are generally thought to have been men of modern appearance. In Europe the Upper Palaeolithic terminates with the final retreat of the ice sheets at 10,000 BP, but this is not the case in other areas. For further details see J.E. Pfeiffer, *The Emergence of Man*, London, 1970.

the two types present an interesting series of problems which are discussed further on p.126. The basis of the Mousterian culture is the manufacture of flake tools, flakes of stone (flint, where it was available, and harder stones where it was not) retouched on one or more edges to make a range of tools including scrapers, small handaxes, borers, awls, knives and saws. The different varieties of the Mousterian, identified through analysis of the tool assemblages (p.35) seem to represent varieties of a single culture-complex, which is often technologically extremely conservative for very long periods of time (p.92). A great deal of work has been done on the Mousterian, but the debate over the significance of the various industries still continues, most authorities now agreeing that they represent the tool-kits of different tribal groups, rather than tools adapted for particular jobs or for work at different seasons of the year. Hybrid industries with mixed Mousterian and Upper Palaeolithic features do exist, as do industries which are atypical due to adaptation to poor raw material or adulteration by later (Upper Palaeolithic) tool types. Neanderthal man used his tools for a wide range of tasks; knives for cutting his meat, hammers and picks to dig graves, awls and saws for working softer materials such as leather.

Neanderthal man was a very proficient hunter, possibly the most proficient the world had yet seen. This resulted in the partial extinction of the cave bear (killed, it would seem, partly for ritual reasons and partly for its fur) and some of the larger herd animals such as the woolly mammoth. This mastery over the environment meant that the climatic environmental limitations which had controlled the regions where earlier forms of man could live no longer applied – some of the Neanderthal sites show that he was capable of living in Europe in conditions of extreme cold, where his remains are found in association with woolly rhinoceros, reindeer, arctic fox, mammoth, wolf and bison. He had fire for warmth and cooking, lived in both open camp-sites (utilising tents) or in caves and rock shelters which were modified to his requirements. His range extended from sub-Saharan Africa to the north of European Russia and the climates in which he lived were as varied then as they are now.

It would seem that by Neanderthal times man had acquired sufficient numerical strength to establish ethnic groups large enough in numbers or importance to necessitate the making of regulations for community life.[4] In the Lower Palaeolithic hominids probably lived in small family groups which would have split in time to form 'daughter' communities further away, keeping the population of any one area relatively stable. Towards the end of the Lower Palaeolithic the expansion of man into vast areas of Eurasia testifies to a great increase in numbers, related to an increased ability to deal with the vicissitudes of the natural environment, a more sophisticated technology and the use of fire. Groups began to combine for hunting, as at the kill sites of Torralba and Ambrona where a large number of hunters had clearly co-operated to drive the game (elephants) into a marshy valley by lighting fires on the surrounding hillsides. Neanderthal man seems to have lived in small hunting bands of about twenty-five, and it is not certain how much contact the bands would have had with one another. In the Upper Palaeolithic increased population led to the varied ethnic groups having more frequent contact and in certain regions such as the Dordogne they seem to have amalgamated into what can only be described as proto-urbanisations.

We are fortunate in that it is with Neanderthal man and the cultural advance for which he was responsible that fossil skeletal remains of man begin to become more abundant. Over a hundred Neanderthal skeletons are known and it would seem that Neanderthal was very widespread in Europe, western Asia and Africa during the period 90,000-35,000 BP. Ritualised burials, care of the sick and wounded, evidence of the practice of 'hunting magic' in ceremonies held in caves – all these testify to the 'humanity' of Neanderthal. We also possess some actual Neanderthal footprints (from the Monte Circeo cave near Rome, p.108), associated with the stump of a torch and a sooty handprint on the wall where the man had crouched in the darkness. Such things bring Neanderthal man alive for us, enabling the formulation of a better picture of early man than we would have been able to obtain from the sparse and often fragmentary fossils of previous eras.

The reason for the relatively rapid disappearance of the 'classic' Neanderthals has given rise to much speculation. Before it was realised that not all Neanderthals were of similar appearance and that less specialised forms often occurred later than more specialised ones the scientific world had envisaged Neanderthal becoming more and more extreme like the dinosaurs, with the result that he was either unable to survive in changing environmental conditions, or else was assimilated or wiped out by an invading population of *Homo sapiens sapiens*. Neither of these hypotheses is now much favoured and it seems best to regard Neanderthal as a form of man which evolved from an unspecialised population at some time during the last interglacial or late in the penultimate glaciation, only extreme forms of which eventually became extinct.

The study of the chronology of the great ice age (or Pleistocene) is complex and a discipline in its own right. It would not be possible to discuss within the space available the various problems in dating material from this period, which was complicated by a series of climatic fluctuations associated with the numerous major and minor advances and retreats of the polar ice sheets. These advances (glacial periods) and retreats (interglacials) are subdivided into minor phases (stadials and interstadials), much work being carried out on the correlation of the various phases in different areas.[5] The evolution of man was thus carried out against a background of wildly fluctuating climate, one of the effects of which was to limit severely the area suitable for habitation until man was sufficiently culturally advanced to overcome such problems. The divisions of the Pleistocene which principally concern us include the penultimate glaciation, referred to in Europe as the Riss, lasting from 200,000-130,000 BP. It was a period which contained many minor fluctuations, and recent suggestions that the general term Riss is being used for a time period which may itself be sub-divided into more than one glacial/interglacial oscillation are probably nearing the truth.[6] During glacial extremes, when the ice sheets extended nearly as far south as the Thames in England, most of Europe not covered by polar ice sheets was covered by local ice caps (as in the Alps) or experienced periglacial conditions.* The Riss-Würm interglacial which followed the Riss was marked by a rise in sea level since much of the water which had been locked in the ice sheets was released, and Europe became covered with grassland and forest in place of tundra. The vegetation history of the Riss-Würm interglacial (130,000-75,000 BP) is known in some detail,[7] as is the transition to the last glaciation (the Würm) which was initiated by another extension of the ice sheets at about 75,000 BP. The minor climatic variations within the Würm are well studied and provide a background both for the final appearance of the 'classic' Neanderthals, their disappearance, and the arrival of anatomically modern man at around 35,000 BP.

Before the Riss Europe had been inhabited by a population of unspecialised type from which few fossils survive. These pre-Neanderthals, makers of the Acheulean hand-axe industries and the Clactonian chopper-tools,† lived in large hunting bands but little is known of their material culture (with the exception of their stone tools) since most of the materials which they used were highly perishable and unlikely to survive the climatic vicissitudes of succeeding periods. However a sharpened stick of yew wood from the English type-site of Clacton has been interpreted as a digging stick or a spear and dated to 300,000 BP, although recent opinion suggests that it might be the remains of a branch gnawed by beavers. Spanish sites show that the men of this time were intelligent and skilled hunters. Fossil remains are sparse but include the Swanscombe and Steinheim fossils (p.25), dated to perhaps 250,000 BP, with low crowned heads, thick brow ridges and cranial capacities of about 1,500 cc. Nothing is known of the tribal organisation or life styles of these people, although attempts have been made to reconstruct their

---

* Periglacial – ground permanently frozen with summer thaw of surface layers only. Tundra vegetation of alpine types of herbs and grasses and small stunted trees such as the dwarf birch (*Betula nana*).

† Acheulean. Called after the site of St Acheul in France, a complex of cultures lasting from at least 600,000-75,000 BP which are typified by handaxes and which predominate over Europe, Africa, the Near East and India etc. during that time. Clactonian. Chopper-tool culture whose chronological relationship to the Acheulean is uncertain. Related to the earlier Oldowan industries.

appearance (p.26). It would seem that they represented the gene-pool of middle-grade unspecialised hominids who were later to evolve into Neanderthal man, *Homo sapiens sapiens* and other divisions of the family tree, and who were the result of an evolutionary process which probably started in Africa at least 5 million years earlier. Fossil evidence of the earliest hominids which seem to be on the road to man comes from sites dated to at least 3 million BP in East and South Africa,[8] bearing the remains of gracile and robust specimens of *Australopithecus*[9] as well as early forms of the genus *Homo* who were sufficiently far advanced to have developed the technique of tool manufacture as a compensation for their lack of teeth or claws and as an aid to survival. The earliest species of *Homo* spread out northwards in succeeding periods, evolving physically and culturally as they went, until by 500,000 BP the makers of the Acheulean and related industries had spread into most parts of the world south of the periglacial zone. With the coming of the Riss glaciation at around 200,000 BP further evidence of man occurs, for example at the early Rissian cave of Tautavel[10] in the foothills of the Pyrenees, where the skeleton of a hunter (markedly similar to Swanscombe and Steinheim) was found associated with flake tools. At the Lazaret cave,[11] inhabited during the late Riss at around 150,000 BP, tents of animal hides had been built over a branched framework, and the skull fragments from Fontéchevade (*c.* 110,000 BP)[12] seem to be more advanced than Tautavel and bear a complex relationship to Neanderthal (p.63). A study of early fossils such as the Ehringsdorf finds (100,000 BP)[13] shows that the Neanderthals were not so very different from their predecessors although they were very different from modern man. The skull from Saccopastore (p.10), was found in 1929 in a stream deposit of the Riss-Würm interglacial dated to about 100,000 BP. It also has Neanderthal features; yet the forehead is steeper and the supraorbital region (eyebrow ridges) not so marked as in many Neanderthals. The upper jaw and the cheek bones are also more delicate.

Anthropologists use the term 'Neanderthal' to describe an evolutionary state where a modern-size brain is packed into an archaic-looking long low skull with a big face. The fact that

3. Location map of sites in western Europe. The shaded area indicates the extent of Figure 22.
1. Clacton 2. Swanscombe 3. Great Pan Farm 4. Spy 5. Engis 6. La Naulette 7. Neanderthal 8. Heidelberg 9. Steinheim 10. Salzgitter-Lebenstadt 11. Ehringsdorf-Weimar 12. Taubach 13. Arcy-sur-Cure 14. Châtelperron 15. Solutré 16. Montsempron 17. Hortus 18. Arago 19. Cueva Morin 20. Torralba 21. Gibraltar 22. Lazaret 23. Torra della Basua 24. Saccopastore 25. Monte Circeo

the brain of Neanderthal man seems to have been, on the average, rather larger than that of modern man is at first sight rather surprising. However it is difficult to equate brain size with intelligence, and it has been suggested that although Neanderthals had a big brain they did not possess the intelligence level that one might expect to go with it.

Stringer[14] notes that the results of multivariate analyses conducted on a number of available Neanderthal crania suggest that the early specimens were morphologically more like modern *Homo sapiens* than the later ones. Reasons for this, and its effect on our interpretation of Neanderthal man as a species, are discussed below (p.24). The same author considers the theories of human evolution which are relevant to the position of Neanderthal man, concluding that four main streams of thought have emerged. The first school[15] sees two distinct lines of human evolution, one (often called the pre-sapiens line) of small-browed skulls which evolved into modern man through such forms as Swanscombe and Fontéchevade. The other line, of more archaic-looking crania, resulted in Neanderthal man via larger-browed forms such as Steinheim. A similar view was taken by the late Louis Leakey[16] who saw a line leading to modern man from *Homo habilis*[17] via fossils from the Omo and Vértesszöllös, with a separate and more archaic line of *Homo erectus* and Neanderthal forms co-existing with the more advanced hominids but eventually dying out, although Leakey admitted the possibility of some interbreeding. A second school of thought[18] saw the early, more generalised, Neanderthals derived from types such as Swanscombe and Steinheim as a likely ancestor for both the 'classic' Neanderthals and the Upper Palaeolithic populations. The Neanderthals underwent an aberrent evolution in Europe, possibly as a result of climatic factors or isolation, but elsewhere modern man evolved from less specialised forms and spread into Europe displacing the 'classic' populations. The third theory[19] which has recently been revived in various forms by anthropologists[20] uses the term Neanderthal to represent populations in various parts of the world which are considered to be morphologically and chronologically intermediate between *Homo erectus* and modern man. Here the Neanderthals are viewed as direct ancestors for more recent populations. Several authors[21] even link the fossil and living populations through polyphyletic 'racial' lines, with, for example, the Neanderthals representing the proto-Caucasoids and Solo man[22] the proto-Australoids. A more reasonable theory is called the 'spectrum hypothesis', which envisages a 'continuity, both temporal and morphological, between the various fossil populations'[23] and a spectrum of *Homo* forms (the unspecialised groups) in the late Pleistocene, only some of which evolved into modern man.

The early Neanderthal crania from Saccopastore, Ehringsdorf and Krapina C appear to represent better models for the ancestors of modern man than the classic Neanderthals. It is likely that a widespread but varied early Neanderthal group developed from evolved *Homo erectus* populations in various areas around the Mediterranean. From this stock certain later populations of *Homo sapiens* differentiated. One group retained a basic 'early Neanderthal' cranial form into the Würm, a second group were the 'classic' Neanderthals of the European early Würm and, closely related to them, a Middle Eastern variant. A fourth group (Omo 1, Qafzeh, Skuhl and perhaps Kanjera, p.115) developed a modern cranial form by the beginning of the Würm and occupied areas of north-east Africa and the Middle East. The apparently early arrival of modern man in the Far East and Australia[24] suggests that there may have been other areas where *Homo sapiens* evolved, of which at present nothing is known.

The pre-sapiens theories of the very early appearance of modern man are untenable, as areas such as Europe exhibit a good morphological and chronological record of local evolution from Heidelberg, Petralona, Vértesszöllös, Steinheim, Swanscombe and Arago to both early and classic Neanderthals. Upper Palaeolithic and recent man were not derived from the 'classic' Neanderthals.[25]

One cannot deny that the evolution, life style and disappearance of Neanderthal man *sensu stricto* is a fascinating problem. The succeeding chapters attempt a more detailed characterisation and definition of the term 'Neanderthal' and discuss the viability of the theories concerning his replacement by modern man.

2

Appearance and Reality

The Neander river is a tributary stream of the Rhine near Düsseldorf, flowing through a steep-sided gorge which, in 1856, was being quarried for limestone. Part of a small cave some sixty feet above the floor of the valley had already been blasted away by disinterested workmen before the remains of a skeleton, later to be recognised as the type-fossil of Neanderthal man, were noticed, resulting in the loss of many of the bones.[1] Fortunately the skull-cap, ribs, part of the pelvis and some limb-bones survived and were passed to a local science teacher who thought that they represented some unfortunate washed into the cave by Noah's Flood, a conclusion which initiated decades of speculation concerning the significance and precise nature of the find. The bones were those of a male, aged between forty and fifty, with a distinctive 'primitive' skull form and body shape for which no exact parallels could be found. A professor of anatomy at Bonn thought that the man had been a 'pre-Celtic barbarian'. Another distinguished anatomist suggested that the bowed leg-bones indicated that the man had spent his life on horseback, a delightful hypothesis which was later elaborated to envisage a Mongolian Cossack from the Russian cavalry who, after driving Napoleon back across the Rhine in 1814, had unaccountably deserted and crawled into the Neander cave to die. Even more bizarre suggestions followed and hardly anyone, even geologists of the calibre of Lyell and Huxley, could be brought to admit that the fossil might really be old, far less that it might represent an ancestor of modern man. One French scientist concluded correctly that the man had suffered from rickets and a malformed arm, but then went on to suggest that the resulting pain had made him knot his brows in anguish; the expression becoming ossified and accounting for the heavy brow ridges.[2]

A definitive opinion was given by the much-respected anatomist Rudolf Virchow, who considered the fossil to be a modern *Homo sapiens* who had suffered from rickets and arthritis along with a severe blow on the head. There was, after all, a blank field for speculation as no previous fossil men had been recognised, the theories of evolution were in their infancy and not believed by many people, even scholars. Society at the time was ultra-conservative and had already decided that a 'missing link', or any ancient form of man must of necessity resemble modern man or be contrary to biblical teaching. People were not prepared to admit the possibility of an apelike ancestor and in this case there was no supporting evidence such as association with stone tools or an extinct fauna to suggest great antiquity. Even with the find of similar skeletons at Spy (Belgium) in 1886 the vision of an ancestor approaching Tacitus' 'noble savage' had not been discarded.[3] A resemblance between one of the Spy fossils and the man from the Neanderthal was dismissed as being coincidental, but the associated tools and fauna at Spy were proof of its great age. A compromise was reached whereby the skeletons were admitted to be fossil men but denied a place in human ancestry. However, the climate of opinion was changing and the series of later finds of Neanderthal remains from the rich cave deposits of the Dordogne (for example at La Chapelle-aux-Saints 1908, Le Moustier (1)* 1908, (2) 1914, La Ferrassie (1) 1909, (2) 1910, (3), (4)a, (4)b 1912, (5) 1920, (6) 1921, and La Quina necessitated a re-appraisal. But the fight over the definition, appearance and evolutionary position of Neanderthal man continues and although over a hundred additional finds have been made scientific opinion is just as badly divided, if better informed.[4]

The relatively complete skeleton of the adult male Neanderthal from La Chapelle-aux-Saints (Corrèze, France)

---

* Bracketed numbers are the notation for the skeleton as recorded in Oakley, Campbell and Mollison, *Catalogue of Fossil Hominids*, 1971.

was used by the French palaeontologist Marcellin Boule in a misleading reconstruction of the appearance of Neanderthal man which warped scientific thought for the next half century.[5] Boule reconstructed the fossil to resemble an ape, misarranging the foot bones so that the big toe diverged from its fellows like an opposable thumb, causing the creature to walk on the outer edge of his feet. The knee joint was reconstructed in such a way that he could not have fully extended the leg and must have walked (or rather shambled) bent-kneed. The spinal column lacked the curves enabling him to stand fully erect and the head was placed so far forward on the neck that he would have been a hunchback. The reconstruction (Fig.4) shows a centre of gravity located in front of the centre of support, with the result that he would have fallen flat on his face if he had attempted to walk, and textbook illustrations of the period tend to show him taking a long stride forward in order to obviate this problem. The three-volume conclusions of Boule (1911-13) are a monument to the influence of prejudice over logic and succeeded in convincing the world that Neanderthal man could not have been an ancestor of modern man and was, as Boule thought, an aberrent species of *Homo* which had long been extinct.[6]

Boule did, however, recognise some of the important distinguishing features of the La Chapelle Neanderthal but interpreted them wrongly. He saw that Neanderthal man was short and stocky, that he had a large flattened head with a protruding face and heavy continuous brow ridges. The robust, chinless jaw was also noted, as were the large eye sockets and bulky teeth. He calculated the cranial capacity at around 1450 cc, but concluded that the shape of the skull showed so many apelike characteristics that the Neanderthal mental processes must of necessity have been 'purement végétatives ou bestiales'. He did, however, suggest quite reasonably that many of these distinctive characteristics were the result of specialised physiological adaptation, and that it was difficult to distinguish between these and genuinely 'primitive' features. He admitted the possibility of chronological overlap and indeed of interbreeding between Neanderthal and *Homo sapiens* but said that this was

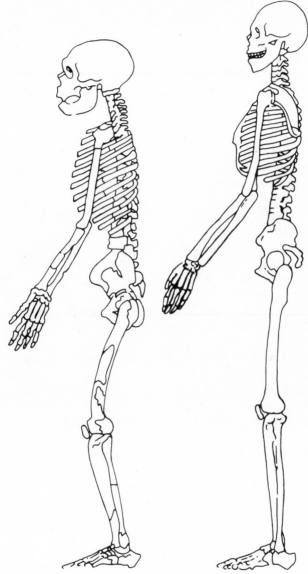

4. Reconstruction of the skeleton of the La Chapelle Neanderthal (after Boule) compared with a reconstruction of the skeleton of *Homo sapiens sapiens*.

'accidental' and 'without affect on the argument that *Homo sapiens sapiens* cannot be considered as a direct descendant, even modified, of *Homo neanderthalensis*'.[6]

A re-examination of the same skeleton by Strauss and Cave in 1957 finally demolished Boule's theories.[7] They found that the remains were indeed those of an 'old' man, aged perhaps forty to fifty, but atypical since he had suffered from chronic arthritis of the jaws, spine and legs. They concluded that there was no evidence to suggest that the posture of Neanderthal man differed at all from modern man, nor was the foot prehensile. The spine was properly curved and the head held upright on the neck (Fig. 4).

A superficial examination of the crania of a cross-section of one's neighbours will reveal many with a distinctly 'neanderthaloid' profile. The popular image has not, unfortunately, yet caught up with science and the model for the popular 'Flintstones' cartoon is still, alas, Neanderthal.

The definition, and reason for the morphological uniqueness of the Neanderthals, has provided a rich field for speculation. Brothwell[8] has suggested reasons supporting the development of a new form of climate-adapted robustness, but wisely ends his argument with the proviso that this needs support from modern growth studies. However the number of theories advanced to account for the characteristic Neanderthal appearance is legion, some bizarre and some credible, but all open to question due to small sample size and lack of comparative material. The theory that the distinctive Neanderthaloid facial characteristics represent adaptation to a cold environment is one that has met with much favour,[9] and many people have pointed out that the short, stocky Neanderthal body was well adapted to conserve heat. Eskimos have a similar physique but earlier people such as Upper Palaeolithic Cro-Magnon man who were living under equally severe conditions show none of these features.* The nose of

---

* Cro-Magnon man. Anatomically modern man was first recognised from excavation at the Cro-Magnon shelter in Les Eyzies, Dordogne, France. He was associated with Upper Palaeolithic tool-kits made on blades, technological advances such as the development of bone, wood, and antler tools, new materials and art styles, and a new social structure.

Neanderthal man, as well as it can be reproduced from skeletal evidence, seems to have been large. A small nose would have been a better adaptation to a cold climate unless the very large nasal sinuses noted by Coon,[10] seven times bigger than those of modern man, acted as a kind of air-warming device. The very large Neanderthal face automatically involves a large nasal aperture.

The computerised multivariate analysis of a number of available Neanderthal crania carried out by Stringer suggested that the early specimens were morphologically more like modern *Homo sapiens* than the later ones, a point discussed more fully on p.122.[11] Functional specialisation has been advocated by various anthropologists, based on the arguments that the Neanderthal diet required large strong teeth and that the brow ridges helped to anchor the chewing muscles involved, the protruding back of the skull counterbalancing the big face.[12] There have been many attempts to reconstruct the facial appearance of Neanderthal man with varied (and limited) success. By far the most convincing reconstruction is that produced by the Russian anthropologist Mikhail Gerasimov, who specialised in reconstructing faces from skull bones and applied his techniques to problems as varied as the appearance of historical characters including Ivan the Terrible and the solution of a number of murder-mysteries. Some of his most spectacular work was carried out on the skeletal remains of early man, a difficult task, since when working with historical subjects it was possible to check accuracy with X-rays, photographs or portraits, but for early man the eyes, mouth and ears which consist largely of soft tissue meant that any reconstruction must be to a large degree speculative. The work of face-modelling was carried out in two stages, beginning with a reproduction of the head itself, with special care being paid to the important masticatory muscles of the neck and shoulder which are highly individual in size, form and volume. This was followed by modelling of the facial mask, a process requiring long training and much cross-checking with modern examples. Gerasimov successfully used his method for *Australopithecus* and for the Steinheim skull, which he considered to be that of a woman.[13] She had cheek bones quite different to those of Neanderthal and bearing a close resemblance to modern man. One of the Neanderthal heads which he produced, based on the skeletal remains of a youth from Le Moustier, is amazingly lifelike, especially when compared with the reconstructions of Solger, who used the same skeleton as a model to make an adult of the same species, or those of Martin and Eggeling who in 1913 made two completely different Neanderthals from the La Chapelle skeleton.

There have been many attempts to define what is meant by a 'Neanderthal' or a 'Neanderthal face', notably those using cultural or chronological criteria. One anthropologist defined Neanderthal man as 'the man of the Mousterian culture prior to the reduction in form and dimension of the Middle Pleistocene face',[14] but this is unacceptable as there are examples (Qafzeh, p.122) where anatomically modern skeletal remains are associated with an early Mousterian industry.[15] Brose and Wolpoff[16] defined 'Neanderthal' as 'all hominid species within the time span from the end of the Riss to the appearance of anatomically modern *Homo sapiens*', which is equally unsatisfactory since the Qafzeh and Omo 1 skeletons are early Würm in date, anatomically modern and antedate many 'classic' Neanderthals from Europe. Stringer remarked on the extreme diversity of the fossil material which he measured, commenting on the relative homogeneity of Upper Palaeolithic and recent man compared with the Neanderthal forms. Within the Neanderthal group itself considerable differences existed, and the classic Neanderthal crania were very different from others such as Skuhl 5, Amud, and Djebel Ighoud (p.121). The Middle Eastern Neanderthals such as Amud, Tabun, and Shanidar (p.94) shared more of the 'classic' western European features, which could have been obtained by parallel evolution or from a common population.[17] The 'classic' Neanderthal face was different from all the other Pleistocene material except that from the Middle East, although Qafzeh 6[18] showed that a modern face shape had appeared before the Upper Palaeolithic.

The best basis for defining what is meant by 'Neanderthal'

5. Location of sites in eastern Europe and the Near East. The rectangle
    indicates the area covered by Figure 19.
    1. Ganovece   2. Subalyuk   3. Erd   4. Vérteszöllös   5. Krapina
    6. Petralona   7. Ksar Akil   8. Mount Carmel caves   9. Amud
    10. Qafzeh

still seems to be the morphological descriptions of relatively early workers,[19] which were largely confirmed by cranial measurements. The Neanderthal cranium is anatomically long and low, with a small development of the mastoid process, and a large bistephanic breadth, supraorbital projection, maximum cranial breadth, foramen magnum length and cranial volume; the latter particularly in specimens that are thought to be male.[20] In terms of the cranial height, parietal and occipital dimensions and reduced biauricular and palatal size the Neanderthal crania were to some extent intermediate between earlier and anatomically modern heads, although Ehringsdorf, Swanscombe and Saccopastore were in some respects closer to modern man.

The phenomenon of *neoteny* or paedomorphism (retention of juvenile features into adult life), has often been mentioned in connection with human evolution,[21] and many scientists accept the possibility that neotenous mutations occurred at various stages during the process, perhaps as early as the more gracile forms of *Australopithecus*. The opposite evolutionary equivalent is *hypermorphy*, also controlled by secretions of hormones from glands, which can lead to acromegalic features, such as giantism and also, possibly, to the Neanderthaloid body structure. The process is complex and a result of irregularities of the pituitary gland which alters the balance of hormone secretion and growth patterns. It seems to be an adaptation to cold, which would fit well with the climatic conditions known to have existed at the time of development of the early Neanderthals. By the same token Collins (1976) considers that it is neotenous processes which result in the rapid evolution of *Homo sapiens* from Neanderthal man during the early stages of the Würm (p.126). If we accept that neoteny was an important process in the evolution of hominids,[22] it seems equally reasonable to suppose that other developmental variations could have occurred, with the emergence of growth patterns different from the mainline trend leading to modern man. Brothwell imagines a case in which there was survival value in reducing longitudinal growth by attaining maximum body robustness and muscularity as soon as possible, which might have been useful as an adaptation to cold Pleistocene environments. If the gene-controlled growth variation within a population was such that selection could act at the level of glandular structures and secretions then endocrine micro-evolution would have resulted. In the case of Neanderthal it is possible that growth changes especially centred on the particularly receptive zones at the bone epiphyses,* and at the growth sensitive cranial base and face. In the Neanderthal children available for study the Teshik-Tash child (aged ten or eleven) has various characteristically Neanderthal features whereas the much younger children from Starosel'e and Pech de l'Aze are more like modern children of comparable age. This would indicate that the growth processes resulting in the Neanderthal features were especially in operation just before puberty. If the sex gland function in Neanderthal had accelerated growth and maturation and the time needed for growth was the same as that in the present day a population with a very different physique from our own would have resulted. In the case of precocious puberty today there is strong growth with early muscle and robust bone development, premature epiphyseal closure (and thus relatively shorter limb proportions) small robust hands and strong hirsutism.[23] If this occurred as a normal pattern in an early population the people would be muscular but not tall as a result of early epiphyseal fusion. But if the total growth period was still of the order of twenty years further joint growth and size increase might occur and strong growth before puberty would affect facial and cranial base development resulting in a large face and long basio-cranial axis. Taurodontism (p.3) might also be produced. If, following a rapid early growth phase, there was still a long period through adolescence, the further action of growth hormones might have resulted in further 'Neanderthal' changes, for instance an increase in hand robustness, additional changes in the size and prominence of the nasal bridge, and the positioning and size of the lower face and facial sinuses. It is clear that much further work, based on

* A cartilagenous area present at the end of every long-bone on the limbs, on the upper and lower faces of the vertebral bodies and in certain other locations where special processes are required for the attachment of muscles.

modern population studies and further detailed measurements of the available Neanderthal material still remains to be done; but the reason for the physical appearance of Neanderthal man seems likely to remain a subject for scientific controversy for some time to come.

The discovery that 'classic' Neanderthal man had a brain capacity which was, on average, greater than that of modern man, precipitated a series of papers concerned with the relationship between brain capacity and intelligence. This relationship appears to be far from straightforward and it is not true to say that the creature with the largest brain size is definitely the most intelligent. Inspection of Table 1 shows that there was a progressive enlargement of the brain from *Australopithecus* to Neanderthal, after which there appears to have been a slight reduction.[24] Although it is difficult to infer psychological development from cerebral volume it would seem that the intellectual possibilities of *Australopithecus* had increased by at least three times by the beginning of the Würm glaciation. The Australopithecines were still very close to the apes and in social behaviour and psychological development there can have been little difference. The greater volume of the Neanderthal brain was probably related to a large development of the centres associated with their powerful musculature. The regions that correspond to the so-called 'intellectual' operations would possibly be less extensive than they are in modern man. Thus the frontal lobe in the fossils from La Quina and La Chapelle only represents 35 per cent of the total surface of the hemisphere, compared with 43 per cent in recent man and 32 per cent in apes. But several present-day people, for example Bushmen and Aborigines, whose way of life requires a very strong musculature, have the smallest brains, but no intellectual difference exists between them and sedentary western European man.

The use of articulate speech played a fundamental role in the development of human societies, and much controversy exists over the speech capacity of Neanderthal man. As early as 1898 Zaborowski suggested that Neanderthal man had 'only a quite rudimentary articulate speech' and this view has been supported by many scholars up to the present day

Table 1

Group	No. studied	Average volume (cc)	Range of variation (cc)
Chimpanzees	144	393	320-480
Gorillas	532	497	340-685
Australopithecines	5	576	450-750
Pithecanthropines	3	871	835-900
Pre-Neanderthal man	2	1175	1070-1280
'Classic' Neanderthal	6	1438	1300-1610
Modern man (racial mean)	–	–	1195-1520

although the matter is still extremely controversial.

Without being capable of hearing sounds in addition to seeing gestures primates, including man, would never be the intensely social animals which they are. Sounds are necessary for contact between groups, scaring away rival groups from a definite territory and to give warning of danger. No other primate save man uses its vocal cords to communicate except on the level of emotive cries, since to transmit abstract thought language is needed. Other primates do not speak because their vocal mechanisms do not permit it, and communication is primarily visual. Earlier human forms could undoubtedly have managed better without speech but it would seem that they too lacked the physical equipment to match the range of modern man.

One of the most eminent authorities on the relationship between the morphology of hominid vocal tracts and their speech capacity is Edmund Crelin of the Yale University School of Medicine. He believes, on the basis of a reconstruction of the vocal tract of the La Chapelle Neanderthal, that Neanderthal man had a fixed single-tube vocal tract which would have severely limited the sounds he could make, and that it is possible to trace the development of this vocal tract from earlier hominids.[25] The Steinheim fossil is especially important in this respect, due to its early date and position in the large gap between earlier forms of the genus *Homo* and the appearance of Neanderthal. The Steinheim skull, discovered in a gravel pit thirty miles south of Stuttgart in 1933, was very distorted and lacked a mandible. Weinert described it in reasonable detail in 1936, and made a superficial reconstruction, and Crelin obtained an accurate cast which formed the basis of his more detailed restoration. He utilised casts of the Swanscombe skull fragments, (p.8) since this is dated to the same period as Steinheim, and the posterior part of the skull is in quite good condition. The vocal tract of Steinheim was similar in size and shape to that of modern man, and Philip Lieberman, Professor of Linguistics at the University of Connecticut, used a computer to analyse the sounds which the vocal tract could produce.[26] Steinheim man seems to have been able to produce all the sounds used in modern articulate speech and over a long period of time this acoustic input or 'encoding' of the brain would have reacted with other sensory inputs to culminate in its functional development, as manifested in articulate speech, language and abstract thought. Surprisingly, Neanderthal man, although much later in date, did not have this capability. Lacking a modern pharynx (throat) he could not form the consonants G and K, nor say the vowels in BAR, BOO, BEEP, BOUGHT. He could only pronounce vowels in English words such as BIT, BAT, BET, BUT giving a narrow range of vocal sounds, not fully articulate speech. There has, however, been much criticism of Lieberman's theories, for example from Professor Catford,[27] who pointed out that Lieberman's data for modern man, 'was drawn only from American-English speakers, and that many modern languages exist with far fewer vocalic distinctions than English'.

In modern man the soft palate, larynx and the nasopharynx are so arranged that a human infant can breathe at the same time as swallowing liquid, an ability which is gradually lost during the first six months after birth. From the end of the first year to the end of the fourth year, there is a descent of the tongue into the neck that results in the loosening of the opening of the larynx into the pharynx, and in the human adult the pharynx serves as a common passageway for air and food. The infant larynx is thus not a miniature of the adult form and as the child develops to the age of four, an increasing amount of the pharynx serves as part of the vocal tract, a

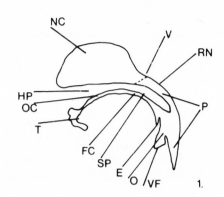

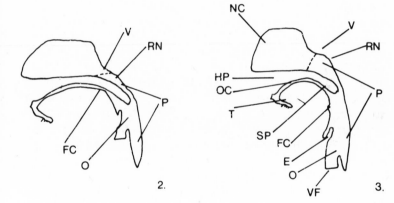

6. Evolution of the vocal tract: supralaryngeal air passages of 1. Newborn
    2. Neanderthal 3. Adult man
    NC – nasal cavity, V – vomer bone, RN – roof of nasopharynx, P –
    pharynx, HP – hard palette, SP – soft palette, OC – oral cavity, T –
    tip of tongue, FC – foramen caecum of tongue, E – epiglottis, O –
    opening of larynx into pharynx, VF – level of vocal folds. After
    Lieberman and Crelin.

recapitulation of what occurred in evolution. The vocal tract of *Australopithecus* was identical to that of a modern ape such as the chimpanzee, neither of which could have reproduced the sounds that make possible the process of speech 'encoding'. The gradual opening of the pharynx as a passageway for sound emitted from the larynx ultimately resulted in a two-tube vocal tract, such as that possessed by Steinheim man. The greater range of sounds produced by the evolving two-tube vocal tract influenced the nervous system and eventually resulted in articulate speech. The vocal tract of the human baby is similar to that of adult apes, and the 'classic' Neanderthal skull base, using La Chapelle man as a model, was much more similar to that of an adult ape or human infant than to modern man (Fig.6). Only man has these unique changes occurring in childhood which enable him to use his throat as part of the vocal tract. Since La Chapelle man could not do this he must have had a very limited language, although this would not have been the case with the more 'advanced' Neanderthals such as Skuhl 5 (p.122), who would have possessed fully articulate speech.[28] If the more extreme and highly specialised Neanderthals also had only rudimentary speech then it may be assumed they were at an evolutionary disadvantage. Could it be that difficulties in communication were responsible for the innate technological conservatism seen in many aspects of the Mousterian culture? If one group of men were able to communicate better than another, then this gave them an immense social advantage in the transmission of acquired information, and in the development of all manifestations of ritual behaviour. In the absence of writing, tribal lore and customs would have been transmitted by oral tradition. No other method of communication can fulfill the same function as speech, unless one is prepared to consider the possibilities of extra-sensory perception which were evoked by William Golding for fictional Neanderthals.[29] Bolinger suggested that a gesture language could have become an equally expressive means of communication, as it is today for the deaf.[30] He assumed that the lower range of possible sounds which Neanderthal could make would preclude his talking very much, since he was not sufficiently intelligent to develop a language from such a limited range. This underestimates the intelligence of Neanderthal man who might have been less capable of articulate speech than we are but was probably just as bright, and it seems that the elaborate sign language postulated by Bolinger would have been unnecessary. It is, however, quite possible that Neanderthal man could have compensated for speech deficiencies by the use of gesture as an ancillary medium of communication.

This possible difficulty with communication raises some interesting problems. In man the specific and automatic hereditary memory which is found to various degrees in all animals is replaced by educated memory which, without eliminating the hereditary memory, delegates it to second place. Everyone has an hereditary memory from birth but it needs to be cultivated by the accumulation of personal experience. If Neanderthal man had problems in communication then the transmission of experience would be difficult, a situation complicated by the lack of overlap between the generations. The gap between Neanderthal man and his more able or advanced contemporaries would rapidly widen to a situation similar to that described by Fred Hoyle in *The Black Cloud*, where the attempt to graft more sophisticated mental processes and a vast store of inherited memory onto simple minds resulted in madness, as the subjects were unable to substitute the new ideas for their old inherited thought processes.[31]

The postcranial bones of extant Neanderthal skeletons have not been the subject of as much study as the skull remnants, but some interesting facts have emerged. Musgrave[32] carried out a multivariate statistical analysis of the bones of Neanderthal hands and suggested that they were morphologically and metrically unique, and that he was not as dextrous as living *Homo sapiens*. Musgrave tested the Neanderthal bones against Upper Palaeolithic[33] and Mesolithic material and a control sample of modern hand bones. He found that the Neanderthal thumb suggests that he had a powerful grip, the voluminous pulp space around the distal end of the phalanx being useful in a cold climate. It seems likely that the thumb was imperfectly opposed to the fingers (man is the only species with an opposable thumb) and the index finger bones indicated that Neanderthal used a rather crude precision grip of the 'pinch' or 'key' kind. Each of the morphological features seen in Neanderthal hands *could* occur in modern hands but they rarely occur together. The Neanderthal hand, completely dissimilar to the hands of Cro-Magnon people, was probably both an environmental adaptation and a manifestation of imperfect manual skill. Could this be the reason that we have so little Mousterian art? The combination of defective manual skills and imperfectly developed speech did not augur well for the continued survival of the more extreme Neanderthals in the gene pool.

A study of the lower limb bones of Pleistocene fossil hominids and modern man concluded that the high frequency of femoral condylar facets (the so-called 'squatting facet' of the ankle) indicates that among the Neanderthals, especially the western European 'classic' forms, squatting was a common position of repose.[34] This is supported by other pieces of anatomical evidence such as the high frequencies of articular extensions at the knee, ankle and subtalar joints, and their marked tibial retroversion. The postcranial Neanderthal bones, especially from the legs, indicate that they were both stocky and robust and lived active lives in which their heavy muscular development would be of the greatest assistance. This active life, which would be expected of such successful hunters, resulted in a number of injuries and diseases which have left evidence behind in the skeletons. The most common disease is rickets, probably attributable to deprivation of sunlight and a diet not rich in vitamins, although it seems likely that children would have been breast fed until at least the age of two to two and a half, as is common in primitive societies today. Arthritis is also very common and arthritic changes are present in the bones from both Krapina and Shanidar (p.94). It used to be thought that both arthritis and dental disease developed with civilisation, but both are at least as prevalent in wild monkeys and apes. Chronic arthritis is especially common in gibbons (17 per cent, in a recent survey) and in Neanderthal it would no doubt be related to the inclemencies of the weather. Dental disease also occurs, especially in the teeth from La Chapelle and Rhodesian man (p.16). Hunting accidents must have been frequent and the presence of a number of well-healed fractures indicates some knowledge of simple anatomy. Accidental injuries must also be represented, although bone-breaking accidents are much less common in man than in other species of primate, where they occur as the result of fights between males and of misjudging the strength of branches.[35] It is indisputable that Neanderthal man cared for the sick and wounded, as is evidenced from the case of the old man at Shanidar (p.95),[36] where one arm is very incompletely formed, containing only a slender proximal part of the humerus. This condition, known as *unilateral pefomelia*, is well known in recent man and has been reported for at least three other species of primate. The willingness of the tribe to support a member who was incapable of working or contributing much to active life must be taken as additional evidence for Neanderthal 'humanity'. One can imagine the old man being the repository of tribal lore and mythology. Evidence suggests that he sat by the fireside doing such tasks as were within his capacity until accidentally killed by a rockfall (p.94). Other primates will also devote some care to sick members of the band, but not at this level, and it is difficult to remove a dead infant from such a group (a phenomenon also observed with larger mammals including elephant). In apes sick or wounded individuals search for caves, niches or just dense foliage in which to die, and this may account for the relatively large amounts of aged hominid fossils which are found in caves and have clearly not been ritually buried. Caves are not places habitually used by primates due to the danger of being trapped by carnivores, although this was probably not true for Neanderthal man whose technology and ability to use fire made him more than a match for predators. Indeed, evidence from sites in the Alps (p.78) indicates that he deliberately sought caves inhabited by bears in order to hunt them.

Hrdlička (1930) thought that he had found traces of initiation rites on a skull from Gibraltar where two of the upper medial incisor teeth were absent long before the time of death, as the result of a blow.[37] This is, of course, no proof of a ritual practice as it could be the result of an accident but such systematic mutilation of teeth certainly does occur in the Mesolithic.[38] At a number of sites there are grooves made on human bone by worked flint to remove the flesh, and skulls and long bones are so fragmented that cannibalism has been suggested. Examples may be seen on the material from Ehringsdorf, Montsempron, La Chaise, and La Quina,[39] and the whole question of ritual mutilation and cannibalism is discussed in Chapter Six.

One of the most frustrating aspects of the study of human palaeontology is that the small number of fossils, often found in a very fragmentary condition, make it impossible to infer matters such as life duration, sex ratios and social organisation. This has been attempted by various authors[40] but all agree that the small available sample size prejudices, if not invalidates, the results. It is really only with 'classic' Neanderthal man that fossil human remains may be used in this way at all. Various attempts have been made to calculate the average life span of Neanderthal, and the results of one such survey are shown in the form of a histogram in Fig.7.[41] The life duration of primates is calculated from tooth eruption in non-adults, and the degree of obliteration of the cranial sutures in adults. Accuracy varies, and a figure of about six months for children and about five years for adults is reasonable for modern man. It is possible that in early populations the calculated ages are too high, although for such an advanced form as Neanderthal the variation is not likely to be very great. Neanderthal man certainly died before modern man, few people passing forty and less than ten per cent reaching fifty. If these figures are higher than the true ages then the difference is enhanced. Neanderthal females (as far as sexual dimorphism can be accurately recognised) tended to die earlier than males, because of the hazards of childbirth. In all the three groups women tended to die before thirty and most men after thirty.[42] The high proportion of children relative to adults must have been even greater in reality, as fragile child skeletons (especially those of

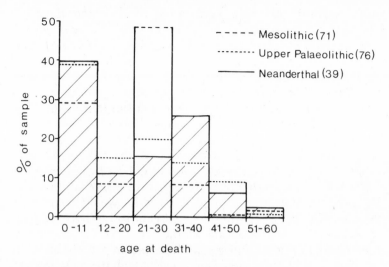

7.   Life expectancy of Neanderthal man (data from Vallois).

neonates*) might easily have been missed in older
excavations. It is suggested that the figures indicate that there
could have only been a brief time of contact between one
generation and the next, and few children would have known
their grandparents. Taking twenty to thirty years as the
maximum period during which a couple could have children
then the youngest members of a family reached adult stage
when their mother had already died and their father would
shortly die. One wonders about the effect of this phenomenon
on the transmission of oral traditions, culture and toolmaking.
Could this be yet another factor assisting in a trend towards
cultural conservatism? In our own society the child learns so
much from its parents, and the effects of deprivation are easily
seen in those families where there is little parent-child
communication. Much family tradition is also vested in
grandparents and, if these mortality figures are even
approximately correct, a growing child would have very little

* Newly-born children.

time to absorb the basic facets of his culture before the death of his parents. Adverse climatic factors must also be taken into account, and it is scarcely surprising that so many aspects of the Mousterian seem to be strangely conservative over almost inconceivable lengths of time.

The suggestion that the development of the more extreme morphological features might be a result of inbreeding must also be considered; although among modern hunters it is customary to marry outside the band, rather than within it, this was probably not the case with Neanderthal. With such a short life-span an adolescent would be forced to mature and reproduce early, and since tribes probably kept to their own hunting territories, it is unlikely that he would wander far afield in search of a bride. Males seem to be more frequent than females in the burials studied, but this is unlikely to correspond to the actual sexual dimorphism of a group due to a number of anthropogenic factors. Were all the members of a group buried, leaving their remains for us to study? Surely men might be more liable to die out hunting and therefore not to receive ritual burial, yet in a patriarchal society one would expect more males to receive exotic burial rites than females. We shall never know about practices such as female infanticide, taboos about the burial of women who had died in childbirth or the existence of other methods of disposing of the dead. It does seem that isolated graves were the rule for both men and women (p.100), but the proportion of the population who received ceremonial burial was only very small. The burial of children indicates that they occupied some definite place in society.

It is interesting to wonder whether the Neanderthals, who probably lived in groups of between ten and thirty, as modern hunters do today, did indeed occupy a definite territory. In Europe the seasonal migration of animals would suggest that the band was unlikely to have a fixed territorial area, since it must follow the food source. However the extreme morphological resemblances between certain groups of Neanderthals (for example the skeletons from La Ferrassie and La Chapelle) suggest the possibility of interbreeding.

3

Tools and Technology

The stone tool industry we call the Mousterian technocomplex, although undoubtedly inferior to the Upper Palaeolithic industries, was superior to the preceding Acheulean. It is characterised by the predominance of flake tools over cores, by a relative dearth of handaxes and by large quantities of scrapers. Upper Palaeolithic features such as blade tools are sometimes found, as is the occasional use of the 'prepared platform' (Levallois) technique for producing flakes and blades. The 'classic' western European Neanderthals are always associated with a Mousterian industry, although it is possible that the makers of at least one Mousterian variant were modern-type men (p.127).

The Mousterian has been the subject of much detailed quantitative work and there is a great fund of available literature. Several basic variants are recognised; the Ferrassie, Quina, Denticulate, Typical Mousterian and the Mousterian of Acheulean Tradition.[1] These are distinguished by technological and typological attributes, present in different degrees within the variants, which are best regarded as parts of a single evolving technocomplex, rather than a series of distinct sub-cultures. Bordes classified the Mousterian tool types into sixty-three different varieties (Table 2), defining types and characterising assemblages by the relative proportions of implements present. An additional list of twenty-one types of handaxe is also used when these are present in the assemblage. Cores, ordinary flakes and blades, flakes obtained from handaxe manufacture and working debris (débitage) are counted apart. For the technological study the implements are divided into Levallois and non-

Levallois types and each of these sub-categories again divided
into flakes, blades and points. Each of the frames is divided
vertically into six columns following the butt type of the flake
(plain, faceted, convex-faceted, convex-dihedral, removed by
retouch, broken or not recognisable). Once the count of
implements in an assemblage is finished percentages are
calculated for each of the sixty-three tool types and a
cumulative graph is drawn up to indicate general trends[2]
(Fig.8). In addition several typological indices are calculated,
the typological Levallois index (TyLI) which expresses the
percentage of Levallois points and flakes not further

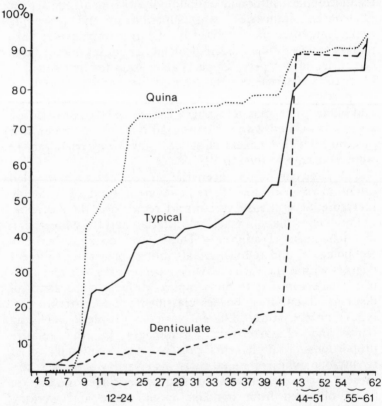

8. Bordes' cumulative percentage diagrams for distinguishing
assemblages (after Bordes).

Table 2. Showing Bordes type numbers and implement descriptions

1	Typical Levallois flake	32	Typical burin
2	Atypical Levallois flake	33	Atypical burin
3	Levallois point	34	Typical piercer
4	Retouched Levallois point	35	Atypical piercer
5	Pseudo-Levallois point	36	Typical backed knife
6	Mousterian point	37	Atypical backed knife
7	Elongated Levallois point	38	Natural backed knife
8	Limace	39	Raclette
9	Single straight racloir	40	Truncated blade
10	Single convex racloir	41	Mousterian tranchet
11	Single concave racloir	42	Notch
12	Double straight racloir	43	Denticulate
13	Double straight/convex racloir	44	Bec burinant alt.
14	Double straight/concave racloir	45	Ventrally retouched piece
15	Double convex racloir	46	Abrupt retouched piece (thin)
16	Double concave racloir	47	Alternate retouched piece (thick)
17	Double convex/concave racloir	48	Abrupt retouched piece (thick)
18	Convergent straight racloir	49	Alternate retouched piece (thin)
19	Convergent convex racloir	50	Bifacially retouched piece
20	Convergent concave racloir	51	Tayac point
21	Offset racloir	52	Notched triangular piece
		53	Pseudo-microburin
22	Straight transverse racloir	54	End notched piece
23	Convex transverse racloir	55	Hachoir
24	Concave transverse racloir	56	Rabot
25	Racloir on ventral surface	57	Tanged point
26	Abrupt retouch racloir	58	Tanged tool
27	Racloir with thinned back	59	Chopper
28	Racloir with bifacial retouch	60	Inverse chopper
29	Alternate retouch racloir	61	Chopping tool
30	Typical end-scraper	62	Divers
31	Atypical end-scraper	63	Leaf shaped bifacial tool

Bordes, in *Bulletin de la Société Préhistoire Française*, 1953, 50, 457-66, gives explanations of all technical terms.

retouched, the scraper index (SI) showing the total percentage of scrapers, the Quina index (QI) showing the percentage of Quina-type scrapers among the scrapers and the backed knife index (called UAI for unifacial Acheulean index) which is the total percentage of types 36 and 37. If there are any handaxes present the handaxe index (HI) is calculated to relate the percentage of handaxes to the total of all the tools. Technical indices include LI, the percentage of Levallois flakes, points and blades, FI, the faceting index or percentage of faceted butts, and FIr, the restricted faceting index or percentage of butts with small facets. All these indices may be expressed as percentage diagrams and these, together with the cumulative graphs, enable the main characteristics of each assemblage to be seen. This has resulted in the division of the Mousterian into a series of groups and subtypes:

Charentian group

This is divided into two subtypes:

(a) *Quina*
The Quina Mousterian is very rich in scrapers, especially of the transverse variety (Fig.11). The Quina index is high and there is an absence, or at best an extreme rarity, of handaxes, together with a very low Levallois index.

(b) *Ferrassie*
This subtype has a very high scraper index but with a relatively low proportion of transverse scrapers. The Quina index is medium but there is a similar absence of handaxes. The Levallois index, by contrast, is high.

Typical Mousterian group

The scraper index of this group is rather variable and seems to divide it into two subtypes. The percentage of transverse scrapers is generally low, as is the Quina index. Backed knives and true handaxes are virtually absent. The Levallois index is rather variable (Fig. 9).

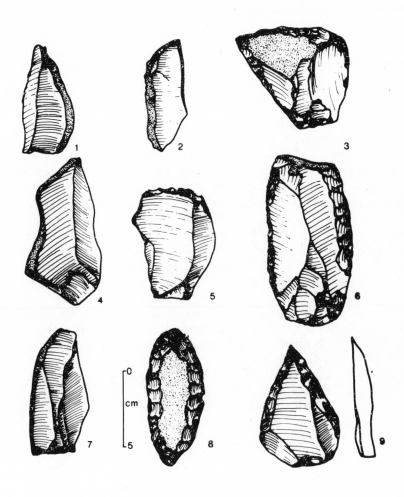

9. A Typical Mousterian assemblage: 1. natural backed knife 2. burin on a blade 3. racloir 4. natural backed knife 5. denticulate 6. double biconvex racloir 7. atypical burin 8. limace with cortex on dorsal face 9. Mousterian point.

Denticulate Mousterian

The Denticulate group has a very low scraper index, often with rather 'degenerate' types. The percentage of denticulates and notches varies between high and very high and there is again an absence of true handaxes or backed knives.

Mousterian of Acheulean Tradition

The Mousterian of Acheulean Tradition (MAT) is one of the most interesting of the Mousterian variants since it is the only one present in Britain. The existence of this variant was first recognised in 1930 and more closely defined by later workers.[3] It is a stoneworking tradition related to the Acheulean and bearing a complex relationship to the Micoquian and Final Acheulean industries.* MAT assemblages are typified by cordiform handaxes (Fig. 12), backed knives and a racloir (scraper: see Table 2) frequency never greater than 50 per cent, together with a comparatively high percentage of denticulate tools. The tradition is divided into MAT type A (with a variable percentage of handaxes and racloirs and many denticulates) and MAT type B (with a low percentage of racloirs,[4] many Levallois points and backed knives). All known occurrences of type B are stratigraphically later than type A, for example at Le Moustier.

The British MAT industries (at any rate in the early phases) are characterised by the presence of flat semi-cordiform handaxes known as the bout coupé type. They may be triangular or D-shaped and are always very well refined, often possessing intrinsic artistic merit (Fig. 10).

Collins[5] identifies the form as his 'Paxton' type, which has an angular butt and straight or convex sides. Even before the existence of definite British Mousterian industries had been established, the connection between the bout coupé handaxe

---

* The Micoquian industries present something of a puzzle. Micoquian is characterised by pointed handaxes of the 'ficron' variety as well as some flake tools. It seems to have been made during the Riss-Würm interglacial and lasted into the Würm, thus co-existing with the Mousterian and with the last phases of the Acheulean. The type of man responsible for these industries has yet to be finally determined.

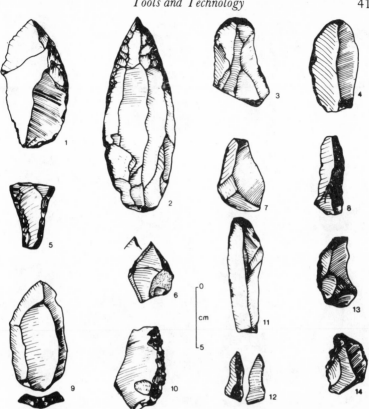

10. A Mousterian of Acheulean Tradition assemblage: 1. simple convex racloir 2. Mousterian point 3. truncated blade 4. backed knife 5. biconvex double racloir 6. burin 7. atypical backed knife 8. backed knife 9. biconvex double racloir 10. burin 11. grattoir 12. backed knife 13. Levallois flake 14. denticulate.

and artefacts of Levallois facies had been realised, and Roe has stated that 'there is a strong case for supposing that the distribution of bout coupé handaxes is mainly a reflection of the movement over open ground of Mousterian man'.[6] Unfortunately many of the bout coupé handaxes are stray surface finds, but wherever the form is associated with an implement assemblage that assemblage is MAT. The bout coupé form acts as a cultural and typological marker for the

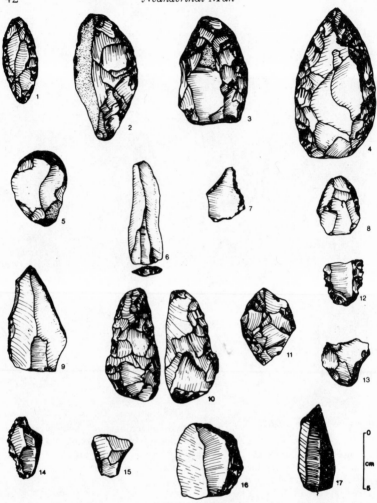

11. Other Mousterian assemblages: 1. limace (Quina) 2. single convex racloir (Quina) 3. single convex racloir (Quina) 4. convergent convex racloir (Ferrassie) 5. grattoir (Quina) 6. Levallois blade (Quina) 7. denticulate (Quina) 8. convergent convex racloir (Ferrassie) 9. racloir (Quina) 10. racloir with bifacial retouch (Quina) 11. convex transversal racloir (Ferrassie) 12. double denticulate (Denticulate) 13. single convex racloir (Ferrassie) 14. denticulate (Denticulate) 15. double convex racloir (Quina) 16. backed knife (Ferrassie) 17. obliquely truncated blade (Typical).

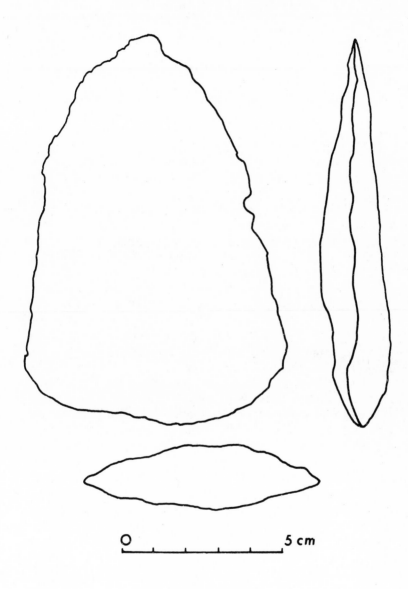

12. Outline of a bout coupé handaxe (Mousterian of Acheulean Tradition).

beginning of the British Mousterian industries, and enables correlations to be made between the rather crude provincial variant of the tradition in Britain and the classic better-made series in France and other parts of north-western Europe. The form is so important because it was made during a relatively short period of time between the late Ipswichian and early Devensian.* No metrical limits or microwear studies have yet been carried out but the state of preservation of most of the examples is excellent. The British bout coupé distribution is patchy, with areas of relatively frequent finds such as in north Kent, south Hampshire, the central Ouse valley and the London area, and within or near each concentration at least one Mousterian site is to be found.

The British MAT sites are poor in comparison with the Continental assemblages but the series of finds stratified within the 7.5 m beach at localities makes an important addition.[7] On the Continent two varieties of the MAT seem to have been made at different periods, the earlier (type A) variant at the beginning of the Würm at the base of the Younger Loess† in France at around 78,000 BP, and the late (type B) close to the end of the Mousterian period in the late Würm 2 (40,000-30,000 BP) which is the 'classic' MAT phase in Périgord. Professor Bordes considers that this type B always succeeds the Würm 1/2 interstadial and that it develops into the Périgordian‡ at about the time of the Würm 2/3 interstadial. The British industries are typologically related to the earlier type A variant and also possess certain characteristics found in the Central European Mousterian industries made early in Würm 1. Archaeological evidence indicates the widespread but sporadic activities of Mousterian man in late Ipswichian and early Devensian times in Britain,

---

* The approximate British equivalents of the Continental Riss-Würm (last) interglacial and the Würm (last) glaciation.

† Loess – a sandy silt formed during periods of intense cold by winds blowing off the polar ice sheets, carrying with them rock debris which had been finely crushed by glacial action. Yellowish in colour and may reach great depths. Several phases of loess deposition are recognised which may be correlated with the Pleistocene sequences.

‡ Périgordian – the first Upper Palaeolothic stone tool culture in France, associated with anatomically modern man.

although the precise correlation of the inland sites is still a matter for speculation. The distribution of finds in occupied caves suggests migrating movements of Mousterian man across southern Britain and it seems likely that more local movements are evidenced by the stray surface finds. At the fringes of the distribution (Mendips, Devon, Derbyshire and Wales) the Mousterian handaxes are poor and often reworked lumps of flint and chert. Perhaps a rather short-lived occupation of Britain by only a few small hunting bands is indicated.

Controversy exists at present over the significance of the various industries. One school of thought, following Bordes,[8] views the industries as the products of different cultural traditions with culture groups co-existing in the same area but having different tool-making traditions. The second school holds the view that the different assemblages themselves represent specialised activities or activity complexes.[9] The major variants have already been described and others exist in different parts of the world. There are also industries (for example those from the high Alpine sites, p.73) which are technically 'impoverished' and seem to represent a response to the needs of a particular job rather than a fully developed tool kit. In some cases the Mousterian variant present is anomalous due to deficient raw material, as at Teshik-Tash, p.104. Many criticisms of the theories attempting to explain the different Mousterian variants have been offered. Bordes' view has been opposed by those who feel that it is unlikely that different cultures could have co-existed in the same area without influencing each other, and that it is equally unlikely that two groups would be occupying the same hunting territory at the same time. However this view can be contended by considering precisely what is meant by 'at the same time'. We tend, as prehistorians, to telescope the past, particularly the remote past, and envisage events which must have happened at different times (perhaps separated by as much as a hundred years) as having happened simultaneously. The degree of accuracy with which we can date events belonging to the period of Neanderthal man is comparatively rough, so it is generally very difficult to distinguish events separated by a relatively short period of *geological* time. In many cases the makers of different Mousterian cultures living on neighbouring sites might not have been contemporary at all, but separated by a period of time which is archaeologically invisible. However, one interesting case occurs at Combe Grenal (Dordogne) where there seems little doubt that the shelter was occupied by the makers of the Typical Mousterian during Würm 1 while a sequence of Typical-Denticulate-Typical Mousterian occurred at nearby Pech de l'Aze. Thus the Denticulate Mousterians of the latter site must have been at least partly contemporary with the Typical Mousterians of the former. Bordes suggests that although the two shelters are close they are separated by the Dordogne river, which may have acted as a barrier between two hunting territories.

There seems to be no possibility that the different Mousterian cultures represent a technological evolution, since they are often interstratified. An alternative suggestion that each type of Mousterian assemblage corresponds to a different seasonal activity is marginally more feasible. However in many cases there are very thick occupation layers indicating continuous occupation over a considerable period of time, without the changes in tool-making traditions which would have been expected had the theory been true. The Binfords suggested, after detailed statistical analyses, that the different Mousterian industries represent different activities following the specialisation of the site. Yet there are methodological problems and it is often difficult to see precisely what the tool kits were used for. Specialised tool kits used for particular purposes and corresponding to different activities are already known from within the same site. Were the Binfords' theory correct different assemblages would be expected from open sites and caves, and this does not seem to be the case. The most likely explanation is that the makers of the Mousterian industries were performing the same jobs in the same ways but with different tools, just as the fashion in tool-kits changes rapidly in modern times (witness changes in kitchen equipment). In this case it would seem that the difference is far more likely to have been cultural and that we must envisage different groups of hunters using different tools, the designs of which remained virtually standard within the group and are a monument to Neanderthal man's extreme cultural conservatism.

The artefact assemblage from the cave of Teshik-Tash (p.94) is of particular interest, since it includes a series of tools made of igneous and metamorphic rocks and semi-precious stones. The majority of the tools are made of a fine-grained dark grey siliceous limestone which occurs in bands in the local Jurassic limestone. It is hard but flakes easily being both compact and homogeneous. One assumes that the Neanderthal occupants of the cave obtained it directly from outcrops, but they also utilised water-rolled pebbles of the same material.[10] Other varieties of limestone were also used together with water-rolled pebbles of jasper, quartz, quartzite, flint and volcanic rocks. The jasper flakes, quartzite and igneous rocks were utilised down to the last scraps and these were carefully saved to make very small points and scrapers (the best tools in the assemblage) which required the most careful secondary working. No cores of green jasper or quartzite were found, suggesting that they had been entirely used up, and even the broken pieces of artefacts made from these materials were re-used and made into small scrapers. The industries from the different horizons in the cave seem very similar, consisting of bifacial discoidal cores, choppers and handaxe-type tools. Flakes accounted for over 41 per cent of all the worked artefacts and there was an impressive array of various different racloirs and triangular points made of the best material, clearly saved for this purpose. Some bones seem to have been used as flakers for stone tools and there is an awl made from the ulna of a mountain goat. Such selectivity of raw materials is also known from other Mousterian sites. At the MAT site of Great Pan Farm on the Isle of Wight[11] the tool makers selected an attractive speckled black and grey flint which must have been obtained from a quarry in the Chalk some distance away. The site, located at the head of an estuary, yielded very fresh implements stratified in dull coloured flint river gravels and estuarine sand, the colour of the implements presenting a marked contrast.

There is ample evidence to suggest that Neanderthal man used some of these stone tools as knives for cutting his meat. Tooth enamel is often scratched at an angle suggesting that he was predominantly right handed. A survey of several hundred scratched front teeth made in 1950 suggests that meat was clamped between the teeth and the excess cut off with knives.[12] This resulted in the upper left to lower right direction of the scratches. The deduction that the Neanderthals were right handed comes from the theory that they would use the most adept hand for cutting the meat. It has been suggested that the development of 'handiness' is related to the development of speech (p.26), as a result of complex neurological studies investigating the 'cause and effect' basis of movement, and the possibility that Neanderthal man was less manually skilled than *Homo sapiens sapiens* (p.29) has already been discussed.

There can be no doubt that the Neanderthals also used certain tools to make clothes, at least during the colder periods of the Würm and in more northerly regions. There is, however, much room for speculation on the precise tools used for dressing and preparing skins, as little work has yet been done on tool function as opposed to tool typology. The initial skinning of the animal could have been carried out with either core or flake tools, and it has recently been shown that there is unlikely to be a positive correlation between tool size and animal size.[13] Semenov carried out pioneer microwear studies on Upper Palaeolithic flint implements, comparing the marks with experimental reproductions in an attempt to deduce the tool use.[14] He concluded that the Upper Palaeolithic end-scrapers (p.126) were used in particular ways in the flensing of skins, and that the long flakes were both whittling knives and meat knives. Keeley has done a great deal of further work in this field using stereoscopic examination of stone tool microwear, with much experimental replication, and work in distinguishing working traces from natural abrasion has been carried out by the writer.[15] The study undertaken by Kantman[16] attempted, by making copies, to study the difference between intentional damage and utilisation retouch on Mousterian notches, denticulates and raclettes.[17] His study was, however, essentially macroscopic and he worked only with utilisation tests involving the sawing and scraping of wood and bone. There has, however, been a great deal of interest in microwear in recent years but much of the work has been carried out in a rather unscientific manner. As Keeley points out, although it is a necessary step to establish that a particular use pattern present on an archaeological artefact can be replicated by a known process (for example sawing) this does not guarantee that the same method of use (sawing) on another type of material will produce identical wear traces. Kantman's 1971 experiment suggested that it was extremely difficult to distinguish between the wear arising from the sawing or scraping of bone and the same process on wood, yet archaeologically this is a vital distinction. It is also important to relate such experiments to the environmental conditions and available raw materials of the site or culture being studied. For example the wear patterns produced by the butchering of frozen meat will probably differ from those produced by cutting fresh meat. Gould, Koster, and Sontz attempted to identify certain scrapers of the Quina Mousterian variant as woodworking tools, on the basis of an ethnographic study of Australian aboriginal woodworking.[18] Studying chert and quartzite adzes, which they had the opportunity to observe first-hand being used to work *Mulga* wood, they observed 'an irregular series of small terminated flakes along the bulbar face of the working edge'.[19] This wear pattern was confirmed by laboratory experiment and the investigators then went on to examine Quina flint scrapers where similar scars were to be found. Although the raw material was not similar it was suggested that these might also be woodworking tools. The hypothesis was disturbed by Binford[20] who observed that hardwoods would have been very scarce in France during much of the Mousterian. The later proposal that the Quina scrapers might be bone-working tools is also trumped by the paucity of worked bone debris from the West European Mousterian, except perhaps in its final stages when Quina-type scrapers are relatively common.

Studies of the animal bone material from caves suggest that bone and similar materials were only utilised to a very limited extent for the manufacture of artefacts, and that Neanderthal man had not grasped the full potential of bone as a material for tools. Of the 6,000 odd fragments of the long bones of the wild ass from Starosel'e (p.89) hardly more than 250 showed any signs of use and none had been artificially shaped into tools. The main purpose for which bone was used was for trimming flakes, and the bones chosen included splinters from fairly stout long bones as well as complete phalanges whose shape would afford a good grip.

Neither bone nor antler was used for the manufacture of precision tools like the needle, meaning that clothing had to be made by the clumsier method of boring holes with an awl and lacing the edges together. At Teshik-Tash, however, there is evidence to suggest that bones were used as fabricators and the same site yielded one pointed bone artefact, made from the ulna of a mountain goat, which had been used as an awl. Similar awls were found at Arcy-sur-Cure which seem to have been used in the manufacture of skin clothing.[21] At Cueva Morin (p.67) Freeman describes a large series of deliberately flaked bone artefacts.[22] These seem to have been weathered before flaking as part of the manufacturing process, and it was suggested that the pile of fresh bone debris had been exposed on the surface for several seasons (up to a full year), in a climate analogous to that of present day Milwaukee. Since cave hyaenas seem to have been very active on the site it seems unlikely that the stockpile was allowed to weather unguarded, which suggests either regular visits or continuous occupation. The layer in which the bone tools was found is a very thick one supporting the latter suggestion. There is, of course, the alternative possibility that the bones were weathered above ground on some form of scaffolding. Very little work has as yet been done on bone taphonomy,* resulting in a paucity of comparative material.[23]

The reluctance to employ bone as a raw material is perhaps surprising since there are suggestions that it may indeed have been the earliest raw material utilised by hominids. Professor Brain postulated an 'osteodontokeratic' industry fabricated by

---

* The study of the relationship between bone assemblages and the sediments in which they are stratified.

Australopithecus in the Transvaal sites, and although this has been much criticised in recent years there is the possibility of some truth in the theory. The Middle Pleistocene kill sites of Torralba and Ambrona (p.10) contain examples of bone pieces which have been flaked and trimmed into tools, and it has been suggested that it was the rarity of suitable stone for tools in the area which produced this adaptation.[24] Bone is a relatively easy raw material to use, readily available in large quantities. If good stone sources were available then the reason for the non-development of large bone tools is explained, yet it seems difficult to account for the non-invention of small implements such as needles or fishing tackle, unless one justifies this by suggesting lack of manual dexterity as a reason for the former, and dislike of fish (p.72) for the latter.

A recent study of bone tools from the Upper Palaeolithic levels of Ksar Akil[25] has shed much light on the techniques of their manufacture. The bone assemblage from the site was divided into awls, points and fragments, the awls being analogous to the borers (*percoirs*) and beaks (*becs*) of the lithic material. The bone tools were seen (by experimental duplication with a wide variety of materials) to have been made by scraping with a variety of flaked stone tools; the raw material (either bone or antler) having often been softened by soaking in water. It is difficult to see why Neanderthal man did not discover this process.

Other materials used as the foundation for Neanderthal technology are few in number. In the Mousterian sites of the Negev desert (Israel) the remains of ostrich eggshells are found in association with Mousterian tools, suggesting that their owners were using the large shells as water containers in a way similar to that used by the Bushmen in the Kalahari up to the present day. Mineral pigments were certainly employed for some kind of painting (p.111) but there is no evidence of the developed styles of painting and sculpture which appear with Upper Palaeolithic man. As Klein pointed out, 'the implication of the absence of undoubted art objects in the Mousterian is not entirely clear, but it may constitute evidence that the Mousterians were biopsychologically distinct from later peoples'.[26] A few 'art' objects are known, but they are primitive and show little of the refined skill and developed aesthetic sense that is present in the Upper Palaeolithic. At Cueva Morin in Spain there are bone fragments with incised macaroni-like patterns, and at Tata in Hungary an ochre-stained polished oval mammoth tooth fragment and a polished fossil nummulite bearing what appears to be an incised cross.[27]

There is, however, no doubt that the Neanderthal technology included the use of fire, without which it would have been impossible to survive the colder periods of the last glaciation. Mousterian layers abound in traces of hearths (p.65). Fire had, of course, been in use for tens of thousands of years before the arrival of Neanderthal man, the first hearths appearing at the Chinese site of Chou K'ou Tien and dating to a phase of the Mindel glaciation.* The fuel burned included antler and bone as well as wood. In Europe the oldest site where fire was known is Torralba (p.10), in association with Middle Acheulean tools; this and other sites suggesting that the Acheulean people were fully conversant with the making and conservation of fire. This last point is of great interest, and it has been suggested that people who used fire may have been ignorant of how to make it and conserved it simply by never letting it go out. Such an idea was explored by William Golding who describes his (fictional) last Neanderthals as hoarding fire which had become virtually a sacred symbol as it was so vital for life. Oakley[28] quotes the story of one Northampton family a few years ago who boasted that the peat fire in their cottage had not been allowed to go out for 200 years. Neanderthal man was, however, a fire producer as well as a fire conserver. Iron pyrites and flint (or quartz) were used to produce the fire, nodules of the former having been found in Mousterian layer 15 of the Grotte d'Hyene at Arcy,[29] and abraded nodules in various Upper Palaeolithic sites. Dried fungus may well have been used as tinder and fragments of the fungus *Fomes fomentarius* were found in occupation debris at the

---

* Mindel. The glaciation preceding the Riss complex, from which it is separated by the long Mindel-Riss interglacial.

Mousterian site of Salzgitter-Lebenstadt in Germany.[30] This same fungus turns up at the Mesolithic site of Star Carr in Yorkshire in actual association with iron pyrites. Oakley suggests that frictional methods of producing fire were probably not used before the development of a bone technology where bone and antler were sawn and ground by the rapid rotation of a drill. Fire, started by the simpler method of striking a spark, must also have been used to drive bears out of their caves, and Blanc reports burnt-out brands on the clay floor of Torra della Basua near Toirano, a scene of a ritualised Neanderthal bear hunt.[31]

Coon argued that Neanderthal man used fire for warmth and protection but not for cooking.[32] He says that in Mousterian layers the long bones of animals had been split to extract marrow while in later Palaeolithic deposits they had been broken in half for the same purpose. It is very difficult to extract marrow from raw bones unless the bones are split lengthways, but after the bone has been cooked the marrow can be sucked out when the bone is cut or broken in half. In European Mousterian sites the proportion of burnt to unburnt bones is just as high as in Upper Palaeolithic levels which makes it difficult to believe that their culinary skills or preferences were very different. Bone was also used as a fuel, as is illustrated by the Sirgenstein cave in Württenberg where charred bones, split and broken for marrow, were the main features of the Mousterian hearths. As no wood charcoal was found it seems reasonable that bones served as fuel, and this feature occurs at other sites.

4

Camps and Caves

One of the most interesting problems associated with Neanderthal man is that presented by his living accommodation, as he seems to have inhabited both cave and open sites on an unsystematic basis, the nature and locality of the site being determined by its designated function or some environmental factor (e.g. proximity to a game trail). Isaac attempted a classification of Lower Pleistocene open-air sites in Africa using their relative quantities of bone debris and stone artefacts as a guide to original function of the site.[1] In a modified form his system is applicable to Mousterian sites, although the situation becomes more complicated with increased technological sophistication (Fig.13). In addition, it would seem that Neanderthal man often utilised his sites (sometimes the same site) for a number of different purposes, varying from short-term visits in the course of a hunting trip to long-term occupation with modification of the cave environment by the erection of structures.[2] Bosinski makes a more useful classification of the Mousterian sites of west central Europe, dividing them into:

1. sites that were used several times and/or for long periods,
2. single ephemeral short-lived camps, and
3. stone-knapping workshops.

This first category includes caves with fixed and limited habitation areas and rich cultural levels (for example Bocksteinschmeide, Germany). It is often difficult to distinguish sites which have been used several times from sites which were occupied for long periods, unless there is clear

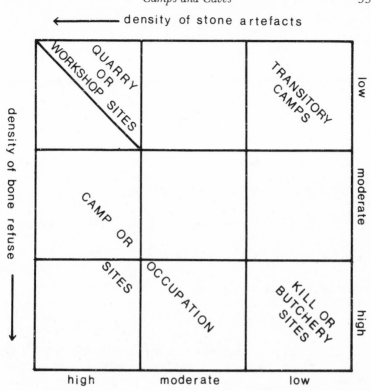

13. Classification of lower Pleistocene open-air sites in Africa (after Isaac).

evidence of seasonality usually provided by the faunal remains. An example of this may occur in open-air sites such as Königsame where there is evidence of seasonal occupation, namely one band visiting the same site several times during the course of a summer. Other examples of repeatedly-inhabited locations are the travertine ('spring limestone') sites of Ehringsdorf and Taubach near Weimar[3] and the loess site of Rheindalen-Ostecke.[4]

Single ephemeral short-lived camps have lesser concentrations of both faunal and artefact material and may occur in caves or out in the open. The raw material for the artefacts is generally uniform and the tools themselves made from a small number of nodules. A high percentage of the objects may be reconstructed from the débitage, as can be seen in an example from Rheindalen Westwand,[5] where the flakes can be fitted together to give the approximate extent of the original nodule. Since the amount of cultural debris occurring on these sites is much less than in the more permanent occupation sites it follows that they are smaller in size, more difficult to find and thus underrepresented in the archaeological record. For every large permanent camp site there must have been many temporary sites of varying size where the group stayed for only a short time, perhaps in the course of their seasonal peregrinations, or where individual hunters stayed whilst out on an expedition. The amount of activities carried out on such sites would have been limited, since operations such as large-scale tool manufacture or the preparation of skins would presumably have been carried out at the home base.

Stone-knapping workshops are only found in areas of suitable raw material. There is reason to suppose that they existed from Lower Pleistocene times and certainly in Acheulean France favoured varieties of raw material were obtained from their sources and widely traded. This suggests that the control of the source areas might well have been vested in one particular band or tribe who would have systematically exploited the resource. But at the other end of the scale there were numerous smaller locations, perhaps an outcrop of chalk with good quality flint, which would have been a regular source of raw material for hunters in the immediate neighbourhood. At these sites most of the debris (at least 95 per cent) consists of cores and flakes and there are few retouched tools. It is unlikely that the sites were inhabited, or at any rate inhabited for longer than a night or two at a time, but they must have soon become widely known. A Central European example is the quartz beds of Hessen (with sites such as Reutersruh, Rörshain and Lenderscheid).[6]

The site of Rheindalen Westwand is particularly interesting since it is one of the few occupation sites examined which are found on the loess. The excavation, carried out between 1964-5, revealed the ground plan of a habitation, namely an oval pit 3.7 x 2.9 m sunk into last interglacial red-brown loess and filled with the light-coloured sediment of the overlying level. At the east end of the pit (which had probably been roofed) was a wide scatter of stone artefacts with many retouched tools, and some burnt flint. In the north-east corner there was a high proportion of cores and large flakes which were only roughly worked, contrasting with the south of the pit which had an area of small waste flakes, presumably indicating that the finer work on the implements was carried out there. One can imagine a small group of people tossing semi-finished implements from one work area to another, rather like a prehistoric production line. Much information could therefore be obtained about the flaking process and the site is known to date to the end of the Riss-Würm (last) inter-glacial or the very early stages of the succeeding (Würm) glaciation.

By contrast Girard excavated a series of Mousterian dwelling structures at Arcy-sur-Cure in France with little evidence of such organisation.[7] However some levels suggested the existence of a cleared area and there was certainly a small hearth, possibly accompanied by a grave trench. One of the most interesting technological features of the site was evidence (only too scarce on Mousterian sites) for the manufacture of bone awls used to make skin clothing.

Undoubtedly the most spectacular series of Middle Palaeolithic open-air dwelling remnants come from sites in the Ukraine, in southern Russia. Here the first early-man sites were recognised in the latter part of the nineteenth century and since then over sixty Mousterian and Upper Palaeolithic sites have been found.[8] In the last interglacial the northern Ukraine (Fig.14) seems to have been covered in a widespread pine-birch forest, although later in the period this gave way to broad-leafed forest of oak and hazel. In the south forest-steppe alternated with deciduous forest; the grassland supporting abundant game. The climatic optimum of the interglacial was followed by a period of apparently rapid climatic deterioration, during which pine and birch made a comeback accompanied by spruce which was very widespread during the last glacial. This climatic deterioration seems to have been no obstacle to human settlement although the early phases of the

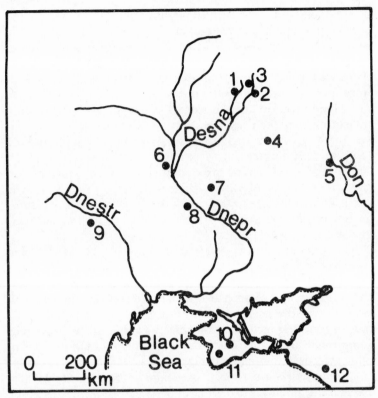

14. Location map of Russian Mousterian sites: 1. Eliseevichi 2. Khotylevo 3. Negotino 4. Ardeevo 5. Kostenki 6. Mezin 7. Gontsy 8. Mezhirich 9. Molodova 10. Kiik-Koba 11. Starosel'e 12. Il'skaia.

Würm seem to have been very cold, evidenced by the presence of plants such as the dwarf birch (*Betula nana*) which is characteristic of north Finland today. After this followed an interstadial with forest-steppe returning. The next interval, the early Würm maximum cold, had a vegetation of dry steppe plants with few trees and there are (not surprisingly) no archaeological sites dating to this time either in the Ukraine or nearby. Perhaps the level of cultural development was still insufficient for man to survive under such very harsh conditions. Mousterian sites are, however, found during the early phases of the middle Würm, a long period of fluctuating climate, but during the late middle Würm and the severe climate of the late Würm the sites are Upper Palaeolithic. The faunas associated with the early sites are those which prefer open (as opposed to forested) landscapes which agrees well with the demonstrated presence of forest-steppe vegetation. The commonest animals were those which lived in large herds (mammoth, horse, bison, reindeer) and it is against this background that we have to picture Neanderthal man living, hunting and building settlements. It is the bones of mammoth which are the hallmark of the early sites, and which often led to their discovery. None of the sites represent places where the mammoth were killed and at virtually every site where the mammoth is especially common the bones occur in patterns suggesting that they represent the ruins of structures. Examples of this may be seen at the early Würm sites of Molodova 1 and Molodova 5 on the middle course of the Dnestr river, and on the middle Würm sites of the Dnepr-Desna basin (Fig.14). At both of the former sites late glacial deposits of fine-grained colluvium overlie a river terrace, and at Molodova 1 the colluvium overlies a thick palaeosol containing shells of warmth-loving terrestrial molluscs (especially *Helix pomata*) which is securely assigned to the last interglacial. These fine-grained sands and silts represent reworked loess, originally deflated from the vegetationless areas near the great ice sheet which once covered the northern part of the USSR. At Molodova 5 there is a complex section with multiple soils representing the fluctuating climate of the middle Würm.

Although both the two major drainage systems of the Ukraine and the nearby areas are equally rich in late Würm (Upper Palaeolithic) sites the Dnestr basin is far richer in early and middle Würm (Mousterian) localities. It seems possible that this area was more heavily populated in the early period as environmental conditions were a little milder.

The mammoth bones were used as constructional materials and only a few parts of the skeletons were brought back from the death site (scapula, pelvis, certain long bones, mandibles and skulls). At Molodova 1 (hut 4) there was an oval arrangement of large mammoth bones enclosing an area with much occupation debris (29,000 pieces of flint, many bone fragments, fifteen hearths and a spot of red ochre). Chernysh considers that the structure consisted of skins stretched over a wooden framework,[9] with large bones used to weigh down the edges. At Molodova 5 (hut 11) a similar arrangement was found, a logical response to a region of harsh climate where there is no artificial shelter. The huts must have contained many hearths, evidenced in the archaeological record by well-defined lenses of ash and charcoal, whose thickness varied between 0.5-3.0 cm, oval in plan and from 20 x 40 to 40 x 100 cm in size. Fire would have been a necessity in this climate, for warmth, cooking, smoking skins and meat and hardening spear points. Reindeer and horse bones were also occasionally used in construction (e.g. at Molodova 5 (2)), but there is a vast predominance of mammoth.

Molodova 1 (level 4) has a rough oval of mammoth bones enclosing the occupation area of some 50 square metres. Radiocarbon dating gives a result in excess of 44,000 years BP. The emphasis on the use of mammoth bones in construction was carried to excess by the succeeding Upper Palaeolithic people. At Mezhirich, for example, ninety-five individuals were used for only one home. The greater part of these were young and semi-adult animals and it is impossible to avoid the conclusions that the Mousterian and Upper Palaeolithic hunters must have been partly responsible for the annihilation of the mammoth. The Mezhirich house frame built of mammoth bones and wooden pegs is now restored and in the Palaeontology Museum of the Institute of Zoology, Ukrainian Academy of Science. This must represent a progression of ideas from the simple dwellings of the Neanderthal man.

Only Khotylevo on the Desna gave an artefact assemblage that is clearly of last interglacial age, with unmodified flakes and blades predominating amongst the 90,000 artefacts from the site. The same tool types characterise the early Würm and early middle Würm sites although Mousterian assemblages do show considerable variability. Since the Mousterian sites in the U.S.S.R. are separated by great distances and several thousands of years this is not surprising. As elsewhere the Mousterian is not a single undifferentiated culture but a

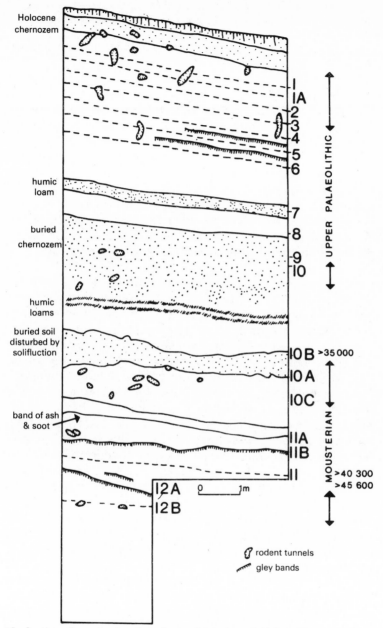

Holocene chernozem

humic loam

buried chernozem

humic loams

buried soil disturbed by solifluction

band of ash & soot

I
IA
2
3
4
5
6

7
8

9
10

10B >35 000
10A
10C
11A
11B
11 >40 300
12A >45 600
12B

UPPER PALAEOLITHIC

MOUSTERIAN

0   1m

ℰ rodent tunnels
gley bands

15. Section through the deposits at Molodova 5 (after Klein). Loams covering the second terrace above the Dnestr floodplain.

complex of cultures ('technocomplex') which share common features (p.35).

The earliest of the Pleistocene occupation sites found anywhere in European Russia date to the end of the last inter-glacial and are roughly 80,000-75,000 years old. Many of the sites included separate occupation levels and the intervals between the successive occupations may in some cases be thousands of years. Most of the Ukrainian sites lie in the major river valleys, not simply because these areas were favoured by early man, but also because the sediments accumulated there, enabling the sites to be preserved.

Caves have, however, provided far more evidence of the domestic habits of Neanderthal man simply because of the preservation factor. Cave deposits are far more likely to survive undisturbed than sites left out in the open air and, possibly more important, caves are obvious choices both for habitation and excavation. Even in Acheulean times the living areas of caves were organised. At the Lazaret cave in Provence (p.10) traces of huts or tents were found, and the excavators even detected where the animal skins used as bedding were placed by noting the position of the small phalanges which had adhered to the skins. Many of the most important Neanderthal cave sites are in the Les Eyzies area of the Dordogne, situated some 300 km south-west of Paris in some of the most beautiful country in the world. Today it is still a region of remote gorges and towering cliffs several hundred feet high, honeycombed by caves many of which have not yet been archaeologically investigated. These caves and rock shelters contain the most important series of Mousterian and Upper Palaeolithic sites in the world (Fig.16). For Neanderthal man the area offered a combination of the natural advantages provided by plenty of shelter, a large quantity of suitable flint for tool manufacture, plenty of drinking water from streams running off the Massif Centrale, and an abundance of game. This resulted in an unparalleled intensity of occupation, and it seems likely that the Dordogne was one of the areas where the 'classic' Neanderthals survived longer than elsewhere. Many of the habitation levels bear witness to the fact that Neanderthal man sometimes modified

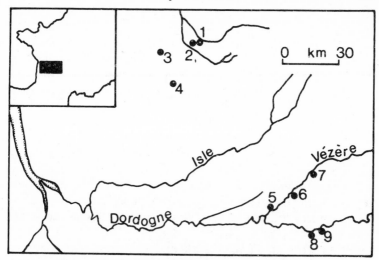

16. Major Mousterian sites in the Dordogne: 1. Fontéchevade 2. La Chaise 3. Petit Puymoyen 4. La Quina 5. La Ferrassie 6. Le Moustier 7. Regourdou 8. Combe Grenal 9. Pech de l'Aze.

the interior of his caves to suit his own requirements. Bordes describes the find of a posthole at the cave site of Combe Grenal, near Sarlat in the Dordogne.[10] On 5 August, 1959, Eugène Bonifay had noticed a greyish circle some 3-4 cm in diameter in the deposits and excavated it very carefully, revealing the posthole. A plaster cast was made of the hole, 206 mm in depth and 38 mm in diameter. The section is roughly circular and the tip, slightly askew, is pointed and penetrated into layer 14 of the deposits. The wooden post, which had been driven hard into the ground, had met stone at this point and 'mushroomed' at the end. Its point had been worked with a flint knife but only the bark had been removed from the shaft, no attempt being made at further shaping. No trace of the posthole was observed in the layers above 14 and the excavator concluded that it had been driven into the ground at the time of the formation of this layer and was the work of the Denticulate Mousterians of layer 14. No other postholes were found but since the area of this one was close to some old workings it is possible that they might have been destroyed before the modern excavations. The posthole must have formed part of a structure, perhaps functioning as a tent pole or part of a screen. Since the faunal and floral evidence from this layer suggests dry steppe conditions and extreme cold such a structure would have been essential to provide some measure of draught exclusion for the occupants of the cave.

Hearths are a more common indicator of occupation. At Pech de l'Aze, also in the Dordogne, two different types of hearth were found. The simplest variety were hearths with just traces of fire, reddened sands and blackened ashes. They are usually small but may be more than 1 m wide and roughly circular in shape. The thinness of the burnt deposits suggests that the fires did not last for very long, and sometimes there are stones around the blackened areas. The second variety, paved hearths, mark the places where fires have been lighted over a pavement of flat stones which has been reddened, and these can reach over 1 square metre in size. The intense reddening of the stones is thought to indicate that they were used for a very long time, perhaps as cooking places where the stones were heated by a hot fire, then brushed clean, and the meat laid on them.[11] Structural features in Pech de l'Aze layer 4 (MAT type A), included a dry-stone wall built in an extension of the south side of the cave and about 30-45 cm wide at the base. Concentrations of implements indicated that the cave had contained distinct working areas, one close to the artificial wall and another near to the wall of the shelter. Study of the faunal remains suggests that during the deposition of layer 4 the cave was occupied at least from May to October, and in the upper levels the cave seems to have been occupied all the year round, although the material from the summer occupations is more abundant than that for the winter.

The Mousterian occupation layers of the Hortus cave (Herault, France) also provide an interesting example of changes in occupation patterns.[12] During the various phases of Würm 2 the cave, which opens onto a steep rocky escarpment, was situated in the natural habitat of the bouquetin (mountain goat). It served as a temporary camp for the

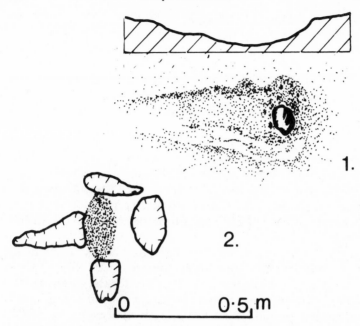

17. Mousterian hearths: 1. section and plan of a 'tailed' hearth 2. small hearth surrounded by stones (after Bordes).

hunters who used the site in several different ways. During phases I and II visits to the cave were only very brief, but during phase III the cave was often inhabited, towards the beginning of winter, as a butchery site. During the end of IVA it served as a hunting camp at the end of winter and beginning of spring and during later phases Neanderthal hunters made temporary encampments under the entrance. The principal game was mountain goat and later cave bear, but the hunters also killed red deer, roe deer, reindeer, bovids, goats, donkeys and some carnivores which were used for their pelts (lion, panther, lynx and fox). During phases I and II the interior of the cave was extremely damp and therefore not suitable for permanent habitation, so that the layers of this date are virtually sterile. However during II the climate was less damp and the presence of hunters is attested by large numbers of bones and tools, including the presence of mountain goat

represented almost exclusively by adult animals which must
have died naturally at the bottom of the great fissure inside the
cave. Plentiful bat remains suggest that human visits were
brief and rare. At the beginning of phase IVB of Würm 2 the
climate of the south of France was much drier, and deposits of
the period are often aeolian (wind-blown) in type. This
change permitted the Neanderthals to bivouac on the ledge
outside the Hortus cave, leaving plentiful remains of their
occupation, although much material must have disappeared
down the scree slope in front of the cave. Fires were lit for
cooking and warmth but the hunters must have been obliged
to fetch water from the valley floor some 200 m below. This
presupposes the use of some form of carrying utensil, perhaps
a wooden vessel or skin bag. Firewood, too, must have been
brought some distance since the immediate neighbourhood of
the cave was not forested. The carnivore bones again suggest
that it was only the skins which were retrieved. The sequence
at Hortus thus provides much evidence for the reconstruction
of the local palaeoenvironment during the various phases of
Würm 2, a period which lasted from approximately 55,000-
35,000 BP terminating in the Würm 2/3 interstadial at about
35,000/34,000 BP.

An interesting structural feature of Middle Palaeolithic date
in Spain comes from Mousterian occupation levels at Cueva
Morin (Santander). The site contains a deep stratigraphy
including nine Mousterian horizons, level 17 (which
contained the remnant) is the third of these strata from the
bottom and therefore one of the earliest Mousterian horizons
on the site. A study of the biotic remains and associated
occupation material suggests that this level dates to a cool
episode within the last phases of the Würm pleniglacial. The
stone tools are a variant of MAT and there is a series of bone
artefacts as well. Intact deposits were excavated over a surface
of 40 square metres, the distribution of all artefacts and
unworked bone debris being accurately plotted. It was found
that the zone of densest stone tool concentration occurred in
17 with a massive partly-cemented bone and tool breccia 5-
20 cm thick. There was a marked colour difference between
the zone of stone-and-breccia concentration which made a

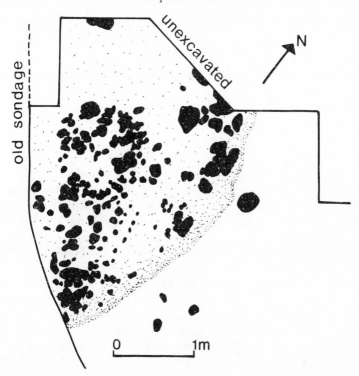

18. A habitation platform from Mousterian level 17, Cueva Morin, Spain (after Freeman).

striking visible boundary, marked by a curved line approximately 3.6 m long and closely approximating to an arc of a circle some 8 m in diameter, although there was not room in the cave for a full circle of this size.[13] A heap of large stones near the boundary was suggested by the excavator to represent either the crumbling remains of a dry-stone wall or else the vestiges of stone piles which had been used to support the base of a curtain wall of some kind, perhaps of skins over a wood framework (Fig.18). The breccia seems to be the intentionally-discarded garbage of people living in the cleaner area of the cave, so the boundary must represent the remains of some structure which separated the heavily utilised dwelling area from the cave interior.

5

Hunting

Neanderthal man was a skilled hunter, the most skilled hunter the world had seen so far. His intelligence and well-developed co-operative instincts helped him to evolve hunting techniques which were so successful that they enabled his people to survive under appallingly severe winter conditions, and which may have resulted or assisted in the gradual extinction of species such as the cave bear (*Ursus arctos*) and the mammoth (*Mammuthus primigenius*). In the severe winters of the early last glaciation the Neanderthals in Europe must have relied on meat, presumably preserved using natural 'deep freezes' of holes in the snow, since plants, roots and berries would have been scarce. Successful hunting probably meant co-operation in bands, as well as a great understanding of the ways of animals. Much reliance was probably placed on ritual 'hunting magic', as is the case with every hunting tribe today, and many people would argue that the function of the later cave paintings was also to ensure an adequate food supply by propitiating the appropriate gods. Presumably Neanderthal man had his own methods but unfortunately he did not record them so graphically. Hunting animals which live as large herds, such as reindeer, horses, mammoth, bison, woolly rhinoceros and aurochs required co-operation, perhaps driving animals over cliffs to their deaths (as certainly happened at the Upper Palaeolithic site of Solutré), or using fire to stampede them into boggy ground (the method used at Torralba and Ambrona). It is likely that he was also an opportunist, catching wounded or sick animals or females about to give birth. Hunting techniques would have to be varied both with the animal and the environment but there is reason to suppose that they included traps, pitfalls and snares for smaller animals (such as hares) and the use of missiles, perhaps spears and bolas. The latter are strips of rawhide of uneven length with stones at the end, which were swung and thrown to tangle round the legs of larger animals to slow them up. Bolas are still used today by Argentinian gauchos who use them to capture cattle. Hunting techniques for large game would probably have been a matter of individual preference and skill, acquired no doubt from earliest childhood. It is probable that there was some sexual differentiation in food-getting roles, women and children hunting smaller game and gathering plant food within easy reach of the home base and the young men hunting large game greater distances away. Constable describes the habits of the Yukaghir, a tribe of Siberian hunters who kill reindeer by chasing them on foot and then summon the women to carry the carcass home.[1] One must hope that such an excess of chauvinism was foreign to Neanderthal man but this seems unlikely.

A band of twenty-five people requires at least 500 lbs of lean meat each week for health, the equivalent of nearly 3 lb per person per day if no other substantial foods are being used. Contrary to what one might imagine by the use of ethnographic parallels the Neanderthals did not always completely eat their kill, and in many cases either their skill was so great or the animals so plentiful that they could afford to carry home only the choicest cuts, leaving the rest of the carcass for scavengers like the hyaena or jackal. In some areas temporary hunting camps have been found indicating that the men of the band ranged some distance away from the main site in search of game. This must often have been an annual event, related to the migrations of reindeer or mammoth in northern Europe or even to the seasonal movements of animals such as the wildebeeste in the south of Africa.

In the coldest periods of the early Würm, in Europe some degree of transhumance would also be required because of the weather. In the winter it would not be practical to live entirely on the open tundra and in the spring there would have been extensive flooding of the areas due to the spring thaw. In the caves of southern France the evidence of reindeer teeth

suggests that the sites were occupied all the year round;
reindeer are born in the spring, so the teeth can be used as a
relatively accurate measure of age. Teeth of many different
ages were recovered suggesting that the animals were killed
during all seasons, (or else that the culling of herds was
indiscriminate). Only inhabitants of very rich lands could
afford not to be nomadic and others would have needed
frequent shifts of camp as the game supply started to dwindle
or as the seasons changed.

Pfeiffer[2] has suggested that in Neanderthal times the
general practice was the killing of single animals by single
bands, and that man had not yet evolved sufficiently to be able
to exist in large bands during severe conditions. Deep snow
would certainly have restricted movement (although there is
no reason to suppose that snowshoes of animal bone and
sinew had not been developed) but one would think that large
co-operative efforts in hunting would be more successful than
small-scale sallies, especially with big game animals. The
advantages of large-scale hunting with several bands joined
together had been realised as early as the Middle Acheulean
and a regression in hunting technique seems unlikely, unless
there was some other environmental factor such as
geographical isolation to be taken into consideration.

Apart from their use as food, animals were also hunted for
their hides, bones and sinews, useful in the manufacture of
clothing, tents, traps and the numerous odds and ends of daily
life. Suitable skins would have been dried and cured and then
softened with animal fats. Clothes could be tailored by cutting
the hides with stone tools and assembling the garment by
lacing with sinews through holes bored with a stone or bone
awl. Since the needle was unknown the finished product was
certainly lacking in elegance but would have been both warm
and hard-wearing. We are, of course, totally ignorant of
Neanderthal fashion but it seems reasonable to assume that
their clothes would have comprised some form of breeches or
tunic, perhaps covered by a cloak, together with a head
covering (perhaps a hood or a rough hat) and something to
protect the feet. There is no reason to suppose that
Neanderthal clothes were as primitive as many illustrations

have made them out to be. Modern hunters often take a pride in their simple garments and there is evidence (p.81) to suggest that Neanderthal was fussy about the quality of fur which he used for clothing. Of course in warmer climates much simpler clothes would have been required, if any at all, but skins were probably still needed as coverings during the cold nights as well as for containers for vegetable food and also, possibly, for water. Hides and skins were also used for the manufacture of tents which is evidenced from Russia (p.60), and indeed the very bones of the animals killed were turned into constructional materials. The remains of ostrich shells on Mousterian sites in the Negev desert suggests that Neanderthal was using them as water containers, as the Bushmen do today. One wonders whether the ostrich was hunted using bolas and what use was made of the exotic feathers. There is no need to suppose that because there is a lack of archaeological evidence for personal adornment no attention was paid to it. It has already been suggested (p.51) that Neanderthal man used mineral pigments as body paints. Ethnographic evidence indicates that many tribes with a very simple material culture have a strongly-developed social hierachy, which may manifest itself in subtle variations of dress such as taboos on the wearing of certain skins by persons lacking a particular status. Indeed this phenomenon is not confined to 'primitive' peoples; one thinks of the mediaeval sumptuary laws. It is not unreasonable to suspect that such sartorial eccentricities began with Neanderthal.

The archaeology of Shanidar cave (p.91) suggests that the Neanderthals had more than a passing knowledge of the medicinal properties of plants. Herbs could be gathered in the right season, dried and stored in leather pouches. Each band probably had its own traditions and a shaman to perform the appropriate rites, and it is unlikely that people living so close to the earth would be unaware of the potential of its products. Plant foods probably made a substantial contribution to the diet, especially in more tropical areas where they are available more or less all the year round, although their importance in the Neanderthal diet remains largely unknown. All non-agricultural people, even Neanderthals, are not necessarily

19. Location of sites in the rest of the world: 1. Shanidar 2. Teshik-Tash 3. Omo 4. Kanjera 5. Olduvai 6. Chou K'ou Tien 7. Solo 8. Ngadong.

exclusively hunters and in present-day 'hunting' communities plants may account for up to 80 per cent of the total calorie intake. Only in extreme arctic or subarctic environments does hunting normally provide the major part of the food supply, and the importance of vegetable foods tends to increase as one moves from pole to equator.[3] Additional sources of food such as snakes, roots, tubers, honey, edible gums, small rodents and insects would probably have been exploited in times of food shortage and, in more severe northern climates, plant foods such as berries would have been stored through the winter in stone or wood containers. Fish and waterfowl remains are not common on Neanderthal sites and one wonders whether this was due to technological problems. Lack of the former almost certainly contributed to Vitamin D deficiency which leads to rickets. In Upper Palaeolithic peoples who had the necessary tools, harpoon, bows and arrows for fishing and fowling, the incidence of rickets is significantly less.

The highest Neanderthal hunting camps in Europe are found at cave sites in the south-east and east Swiss and Austrian Alps. Here the hunters lived in or visited caves situated in south-facing valleys which received a flow of warmer air. Sites such as Repolust, Badl-Höhle and Kugelsteinhöhle situated at below 900 km OD were not true permanent camps but rather temporary hunting stops. It seems unlikely that the hunters were always living in the high mountain zone, and they probably just visited the area in search of game. Should this be the case then the caves were probably occupied during the spring, when groups of people usually living at lower altitudes could visit the high mountains. All the sites have amorphous stone industries which make use of water-rolled pebbles and contain very few flakes, making it almost impossible to relate them to the standard Mousterian divisions already outlined (p.37). They presumably represent tool kits hastily made for particular jobs.[4] The faunas of these hunting camps are dominated by cave bears, but also contain ibex, chamois and more rarely musk ox and small rodents. Sedimentary analysis suggests that many of the caves were frequented during a period of relatively warm climate[5] when the lower limit of the permanent snow cover was about a mile higher than today. It is difficult to decide whether the vast accumulations of cave bear bones indicate active hunting or merely preying upon weak or dead animals, since it is very difficult to distinguish from the skeleton between a bear killed by hunters and a bear dying a natural death. Bandi suggests that the bear bones are the result of the natural accumulation of dead bears, and this conclusion is supported by Gabori-Csank,[6] for both the Swiss Alps and the cave sites in the mountains of eastern Europe. However active hunting did definitely take place, at Crni-kal bear skeletons were distributed according to the parts of the body, which indicates definite hunting specialisation. One wonders about the technique used for bear-hunting. The Eskimos of Alaska hunt the Kodiak bear (*Ursus gigas*) by allowing it to impale itself on a spear held on the ground by a

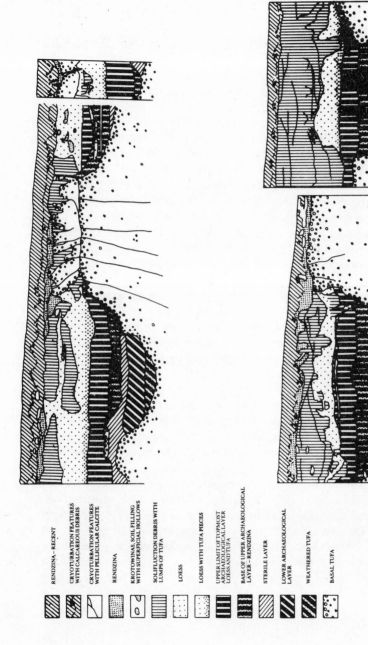

RENDZINA – RECENT

CRYOTURBATION FEATURES WITH CALCAREOUS DEBRIS

CRYOTURBATION FEATURES WITH PELLICULAR CALCITE

RENDZINA

KROTOWINAS, SOIL FILLING WITH SUPERFICIAL HOLLOWS

SOLIFLUCTION DEBRIS WITH LUMPS OF TUFA

LOESS

LOESS WITH TUFA PIECES

UPPER LIMIT OF TOPMOST ARCHAEOLOGICAL LAYER LOESS AND TUFA

BASE OF UPPER ARCHAEOLOGICAL LAYER – RENDZINA

STERILE LAYER

LOWER ARCHAEOLOGICAL LAYER

WEATHERED TUFA

BASAL TUFA

20. Section through the deposits at Erd, Hungary (after Gabori-Csank).

foot placed firmly on the butt. This enables an animal weighing 1800 lbs to be killed by another weighing perhaps 150 lbs. Perhaps Neanderthal man thought of the same idea?

The Hungarian site of Erd is located approximately 25 km south-east of Budapest, on a plateau in the Bükk mountains.[7] It was an open-air site developed at the heads of two small valley-depressions not more than 22 m long, separated by a tufaceous divide. Despite the fact that it is an open-air site the vast preponderance of cave bear in the fauna makes it unique. The habitation area seems to have encompassed all the area of the depressions and the fills can be divided into a series of levels which correlate with various phases of Würm sedimentation. The archaeological layers are divided into two complexes, separated by a sterile layer. Both contain animal bones and implements, and in the lower complex wood charcoal is very well preserved. The stratigraphy of the site is shown in Fig.20, illustrating the complex nature of the fills which bear much evidence of periglacial disturbance and include a thick deposit of loess, capping the archaeological levels which formed during the maximum cold of Würm 1. The reddish-brown fossil soil at the base of the section is of Riss-Würm interglacial date, and both the archaeological levels belong to the early Würm, before the maximum cold, encompassing two minor interstadials. The archaeological layers were thus formed during the long initial phase of Würm 1, during which there were at least nine minor climatic oscillations (the section includes, for example, two thin bands of loess). Below this the charcoal fragments in the buried soil are of species characteristic of the warm Mediterranean climate of the end of the Riss-Würm interglacial, which was followed by the Würm 1 which seems to have been both wet and cold with periodic onsets of periglacial conditions. Charcoal fragments suggest that the fauna surrounding the area was a mixture of deciduous trees such as birch with conifers such as larch, pine, spruce and fir. The population of Scots pine (which dominates in the lower archaeological level) notably decreases with time and that of the larch increases. The different botanical phases correlate neatly with the Würm stratigraphy and add further information to our knowledge of the climate of the time.

The faunal remains include over 50,000 bones of which 15,000 are identifiable. Forty-five species of animal are represented and the composition of the assemblage reflects hunting bias. In the older levels more thermophilous (warmth-loving) species are found but in the upper layers animals such as the arctic fox, reindeer and ibex occur which indicate the colder tundra-like conditions. The microfauna of the upper complex indicates a summer temperature of about 16°C. Dates for the upper complex are: Upper complex (layer d) 35,300 ± 900 (GrN 4443); Upper complex (layer e) 44,300 ± 1400 (GrN 4444).

The stone tool industry is dominated by quartzite of several varieties, the poorest quality of which was used for the largest tools. Many of the implements were made on rolled quartzite pebbles, resulting in flakes of a very distinctive appearance. The implements belong typologically to the Charentian Mousterian and are rather standardised, but without the Levallois technique due to the poor quality of the raw material. Forty-eight varieties of tools were distinguished, mainly consisting of different types of racloirs. Some worked bone and antler was included but the main character of the industry was determined by the fact that it was well adjusted to a raw material of quartzite pebbles.

The smaller depression seems to have served the hunters as a meat store and has large quantities of cave bear bones but relatively few implements. The larger of the depressions was clearly used for occupation, probably on a seasonal basis, and might even have been roofed. The nineteen relatively large animal species which were used for food (and/or pelts) account for 99.7 per cent of the identifiable bones. Medium and small game seem not to have been an important food supply but there is little doubt that the food animals which are represented were obtained by active hunting and not by scavenging dead animals. Towards the end of the occupation of the site the hunters were eating horse, donkey and rhinoceros as well as bear (Fig.21). The cave bear seems to have either been brought to the site whole or killed very nearby, since the proportional representation of the skeletal

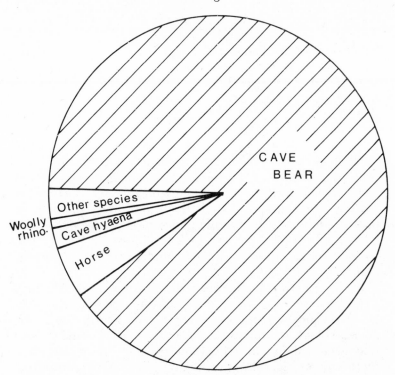

21. Relative proportions of animals killed by the hunters at Erd, showing the overwhelming concentration on cave bear.

parts is correct. This is not so for the other species. Horse, which comprises 44 per cent of the remainder of the fauna, seems to have been represented by only the head and long bones. The bones of between 500-550 cave bears are found, and 180-200 other animals. The cave hyaena which is relatively important in the fauna was probably killed for its pelt. The woolly rhinoceros is also, like the horse, represented by skull-fragments and long bones but there are no vertebrae or flanks. The remains of the brown bear consist principally of phalanges, suggesting that the pelts alone were retrieved and that the animal was not eaten. The nineteen large species (Fig.21) exclude animals such as the marten, varying hare, and boar which are very rare in the fauna. It is clear that these people based their mode of life on the cave bear and it seems strange to kill the bear and then transport it whole to the site. The remains include neonates and small cubs as well as adults. To retrieve the carcass of so large and heavy an animal suggests that it was killed near the camp, while the predominance of terminal bones of the brown bear suggests that the skin arrived without the animal. The horse was probably killed far from the camp and only the head and limbs brought back. The reason for the choice of the head is difficult to understand unless it was to eat the brain or for some ritual reason. The hunters must have accumulated a very large quantity of bear skins and one can but wonder whether this concentration on the bear, surely not the most tasty of animals and certainly difficult and dangerous to kill, has anything to do with this fact. Could the skins have been traded, and if so what did the hunters receive in return? Honey?[8]

In the eastern Alps there is a distinction between the high mountains of the interior and the peripheral zones (archaeologically more important) which is reflected in the palaeoecology and differences in ways of life. During the last interglacial abundant vegetation seems to have developed there even at high altitudes, the deciduous forests favouring the production of a large population of cave bears which seem to have been the dominant species in the area. The temperature at this time was at least 8-10°C higher than the present and the rainfall also greater, perhaps as much as 1,200 mm per year. All the animals present are adapted to the warm forest environment, and after the cave bear the most important species are ibex, chamois, red deer, roe deer and wild boar. The bears lived in quantities in the caves such as Drachenloch at altitudes greater than 200 m. During the early phases of the Würm the upper forest limit was much reduced and at the end of Würm 1 there was a climatic change marked by a change in the fauna, the hunted animals now including mammoth, woolly rhinoceros, horse, reindeer, bison, aurochs and *Asinus hydruntinus*, all of which suggest an increase in tundra at the expense of the forest. Few of the Mousterian sites date to this phase, and the cold continental climate is reflected in extensions of taiga (*larix, picea*, etc.) and coniferous forests at the expense of the deciduous trees.

At Subalyuk there are two complexes of Mousterian levels separated by a thin sterile layer. The site seems to have been inhabited during many different periods but it is difficult to gauge the length of the respective occupations. In the lower (earlier) levels the fauna is dominated by ibex and cave bear, the high proportion of ibex indicating a hunting speciality dating probably to the end of the last interglacial and the beginning of Würm 1.[9] Active hunting of animals such as rhinoceros and horse (which are also well-represented in the fauna) must have been carried out on the plains near the cave and Gabori-Csank[10] calculates that the catchment area for the hunters cannot have exceeded 25 km around the site. In the upper complex the fauna is dominated by cave bear and there are lesser numbers of reindeer, mammoth and horse, indicating colder conditions. The site is remarkable for the small numbers of implements found associated with the fauna – only 200 implements in the lower complex and 300 in the upper – very few when considering that the remains of several hundred animals are represented.

Similar hunting specialisations have been observed at the mammoth hunter sites of the Russian steppes, whose structural remains have already been described (p.60). None of the sites represent places where the mammoth were actually killed and here again only a few parts of the skeleton seem to have been brought home. These, however, included such heavy bones as scapulae, certain long bones, mandibles and tusks which were to serve as constructional materials, and the bones do not represent those parts which gave the greatest meat yield. The labour involved in concentrating the bones at sites was very considerable, since a defleshed and dried mammoth skull with relatively small tusks weighs a minimum of 100 kg and the other bones are also heavy.[11]

It would have been difficult to hunt and kill such large beasts on a regular basis and many, if not all, of the bones were scavenged from animals which had died naturally, in the same manner as the Alpine cave bear sites. Chemical analysis of the bone from Mezin indicates that mammoths of very different geological ages are represented in a single mammoth bone ruin, and it is likely that the Mousterian constructions were themselves scavenged by later builders. The bones were also probably used as fuel, since small pieces of charred bone are very common in the late Würm (Upper Palaeolithic) sites of the Dnepr-Desna basin, an area where palaeobotanical research shows that trees would have been relatively rare, and it is probable that the bones were put to similar use in the earlier period. Most of the reindeer and horse bones found on Russian Mousterian sites have been fractured to facilitate the extraction of the nutritious marrow, and this indicates that, unlike the mammoth, the animals were systematically hunted for food. Modern people such as the Lapps who live under adverse climatic conditions make extensive use of marrow, sucked straight from the bone and extracted to add to 'stews'. There is no reason why Neanderthal man should not have used the bones in a similar way. It is, however, possible that at some of the sites a small proportion of the reindeer remains (especially antlers) were scavenged, since they were used as constructional materials (as at Molodova 5 (2)).[12] The bones of carnivores are relatively rare in the early sites which presumably reflects the rarity of carnivores in the ancient environment and the difficulty of hunting them, especially dangerous ones like the lion or bear. Both the latter were hunted largely for their pelts, as at Erd, and at both Mezin and Ardeevo whole or nearly whole skeletons of these animals were found which possessed everything except their paws, presumably removed with the skin.[13] Separate but articulated paw skeletons are found repeatedly. At Eliseevichi particular age groups of foxes seem to have been hunted, possibly related to the quality of the fur, and Polikarpovitch gives a histogram of the ages. Klein quotes his figures in comparison with the age distribution of modern free-ranging populations (Table 3).[14]

This suggests that the Eliseevichi hunters preferred, and deliberately selected, pelts of middle-aged foxes, rather than young ones, although these would have been more common in a normal population. At some sites, for example Gontsy, hares as well as foxes were utilised for their pelts, and the same

Table 3. Age groups of foxes hunted at Eliseevichi

No. of animals	Age	No. of animals in modern sample
6	less than 8 months	20
16	1 year	7
13	2 years	7
5	3 years	3

pattern of complete skeletons with separate but articulated paws is found.[15] On the early Würm sites of the Dnestr many indicators of cold climate were found; such as the snow lemming (*Dicrostonomyx torquatus*) and the snowy owl (*Nyctea scandiaca*) at Mezin. Game birds were rare, as usual, but the bones of ptarmigan and the snowy partridge occur. The scarcity of wildfowl suggests that the sites were probably occupied in winter when the game birds were far to the south – or else that the Mousterian technology was not sufficiently advanced to catch them. Few fish bones occur, either for reasons already advanced or because to fish in frozen rivers is difficult. It is, indeed, possible that all the known sites represent winter camps built in the comparative shelter of the river valleys, while the as yet unexcavated summer camps were located on the interfluves where the herds of horse, reindeer, bison and mammoth grazed.

At the cave site of Teshik-Tash (p.105) the hunters specialised in the Siberian mountain goat (*Capra siberica*) which forms over 83 per cent of the faunal assemblage recovered, seventy-eight individuals being represented.[16] The wild goats live in the high mountainous gorges up to the snow line, and are skillfully adapted to this dangerous terrain. The hunters must have been both agile and daring and possessed considerable knowledge of the habits of their prey. Not only would the goats have been tricky to hunt but returning to camp heavily laden with meat would itself have required strength and endurance. Movius suggests that the goats were hunted either by rolling stones from above or by ambushes at watering-places. An alternative would be organised drives over the edge of precipices, a method still used in Russia in the nineteenth century by the Kamchadals.[17] Most of the bones are from the leg and all the hooves are missing, suggesting the dismembering of carcasses on site with only the best parts being retrieved. The heads and horns were sometimes collected, probably for ritual reasons (p.104) or the preparation of glue. Of the animals represented in the faunal assemblage the mountain goat, snow leopard and wild horse still live in the area today, only the hyaena now being extinct. The site probably dates to the Central Asiatic equivalent of the Würm/Würm 2 interstadial, although it may be as early as the preceding (Riss/Würm) interglacial. The vegetation around the cave consisted of juniper and mountain plants, with snow patches lasting as long as June/July and sporadic meadows of high Alpine grass. The wild boar and deer were to be found in the lower altitude forest and horses occasionally penetrated into the high meadows from the surrounding steppe.

At Il'skaia, in the northern Caucasus, there was a hunting speciality in bison, the remains of over 600 animals being found at the site.[18] At that time the vegetation of the area would have been a treeless steppe, rather like the prairies of the northern United States, and the bison roamed in great herds providing meat, clothing and the raw materials for tents for their hunters.

It may seem extraordinary to us, accustomed to the infinite dietary variations made available by western civilization, that anyone should choose to subsist on one particular food source, as Neanderthal man clearly often did. However it must always be remembered that the archaeological evidence is dependent on factors such as preservation. Plant foods may have been important, or the Neanderthals might have fished yet eaten their catch away from the site so that the bones did not enter into the deposit. Many features of the Neanderthal way of life suggest extreme conservatism, such as the great thickness of deposit at Shanidar (p.92) with a lithic assemblage virtually unchanged for 40,000 years, and it may be that if one's father and grandfather always hunted bison then one automatically did the same thing without questioning whether other food sources might be as pleasant or indeed more readily available.[19] This seems to be a basic human character trait, which we are still seeing today in the public reluctance to accept soya bean products as meat substitutes or any food that is different in colour or texture from that to which we have become accustomed as being equally nutritious. Could Neanderthal dietary specialisation be yet another piece of evidence for his humanity?

6

Ritual and Burial

Tailhard de Chardin[1] used the term 'hominisation' for the progression from instinct to thought which happened during evolution and whose highest manifestations are to be observed in our own species. Tobias refers to 'cultural hominisation', the dependence of man on cultural mechanisms such as clothing and the control of fire to adapt to any environment.[2] It is incontestable that the degree of hominisation achieved by Neanderthal was much greater than that of previous hominids, and it is with Neanderthal that signs of spiritual in addition to physical evolution manifest themselves. Such features as the systematic burial of the dead, and the appearance of complex rituals involving animal 'totems' persist in some form or another in different cultures right down to the present day. The formulation of ritual behaviour by Neanderthal man is difficult to understand in our own terms, as our mythological legacies exist in the form of written records and verbally-transmitted ideas. We know that Neanderthal did not have the former and the problem of communication required for the latter has already been discussed (p.26). Yet he had definite rituals which probably remained unchanged for considerable periods of time. One must in fairness admit that the importance of ritual behaviour to Neanderthal (measured by the percentage of sites where it is evidenced) was much less than to Upper Palaeolithic man, yet all the Upper Palaeolithic traits which are conventionally considered as the foundations of our cultural heritage (cemetary burial, proto-urbanisation, social stratification, different art forms, care for the sick and wounded) were present in Neanderthal times but in very simple form. Such codes of conduct generated by spiritual evolution have now come to dominate our social life.

Until the time of the discovery of the Mousterian graves at La Ferrassie by Capitan and Peyrony[3] few people believed that Palaeolithic man buried his dead, and this was thought far too 'human' a trait for Neanderthal. But the complex structures at La Ferrassie and their indisputable association with Mousterian artefacts provided refutation of this theory, although the arguments as to the degree of 'humanity' possessed by Neanderthal man continue to this day. The early find of the skeleton of an adolescent Neanderthal at Le Moustier was 'excavated' in 1908 by Hauser in what Vallois described as 'conditions scientifiques déplorables',[4] leaving room for doubt as to whether or not the burial was intentional. Peyrony later found two trenches dug in a Mousterian layer in the same cave;[5] one covered by three flat stones contained fragments of bone and flint. The second included the remains of a very young child buried with stone tools, leaving no doubt that the burial was deliberate, but it had come too late, as in the course of the preceeding year the La Chappelle discovery had been published by Bardon and Bouyssonie[6] and work had been begun by Peyrony at La Ferrassie which was to yield six Neanderthal burials between 1909 and 1921. The initial publication of the La Chappelle find was made in a brief announcement in 1908, and the later (1913) paper was heavily influenced by the discoveries at Le Moustier, La Ferrassie, and Spy.

Bardon and Bouyssonie (1913) synthesised six features of these early discoveries which they thought provided evidence of formal burial:

1. The bent position of the body, as in sleep, to give the most favourable impression of death (La Ferrassie 1 and 2, Le Moustier and Spy).

2. Measures for protecting the body (large flat stones laid on the head at La Chappelle, piles of bone splinters over the stomach at La Ferrassie 1, a flint cover over the Le Moustier head and the nose protected by two flakes).

3. Provision of food (at La Chappelle a beef joint near the right hand and a joint of reindeer a little further away).

4. Well-made flints ('belles pièces') near the body (La Chappelle, Le Moustier, La Ferrassie 3 and 4).

5. Making a grave for the body (La Chappelle, La Ferrassie 3 and 4).

6. 'Magic' role played by certain graves (at La Ferrassie the trench contained the remains of large bovids near burials 3 and 4, and at La Chappelle bison horns had been placed at the cave entrance for 'protection').

Such revolutionary humanitarian ideas were resolutely opposed by members of the 'Old Guard' who persisted for some time in regarding Neanderthal man as a sub-human brute (p.15). However, the discoveries at La Chappelle and La Ferrassie alone really left no room for doubt that intentional graves did exist in the Middle Palaeolithic, although some of their arguments are open to discussion. The notion of 'belles pièces' is debatable since the idea of exceptionally well-made artefacts being left near the body is the result of value judgments which may not be those of Neanderthal. There is little doubt that Neanderthal man did often make pieces whose symmetrical shape and high degree of refinement were greater than would be dictated by purely practical considerations, the bout coupé handaxes (p.43) being a fine example. At La Chappelle there is some doubt as to whether the well-made pieces were actually placed near the body. The Bardon and Bouyssonie arguments which have stood the test of time are the flexed body position and the artificially-dug grave, both of which recur in Neanderthal burials discovered at later dates. Nor is the provision of food for the dead surprising. It would, after all, be callous to leave the dead without sustenance or weapons for his journey and this theme recurs throughout prehistory and lasts sporadically until the onset of Christianity.

The cemetery site of La Ferrassie yielded a stratified series of graves, including the remains of an adult male, a female, two children and three foetus or neonates. There were also several trenches that seem to have been designed as graves but which were empty, possibly because their contents had decomposed or been dug up by the cave hyaena. The man, who was aged about forty-five, was found at the base of the burial layer. The skeleton showed that he had been buried lying on his back, slightly inclined towards the left, with flexed legs. Three flat stones were associated with the burial, one near the skull and the others on the arms, and various incised large bones, bone splinters, and flint flakes had been put on his grave, the former often being interpreted as protection for the burial. Near the male grave was the skeleton of a woman aged between twenty-five and thirty, buried in such a flexed position as to suggest that she might have been tied up before burial. This use of the flexed position is interesting, and is discussed below (p.99). It might be related to the Bardon and Bouyssonie idea of making the dead person look as if he was sleeping, or alternatively it might be an economy measure since a flexed body takes less space and the graves had often to be dug into intractable materials. No grave goods accompanied this burial. Neanderthals 3 and 4 were buried in trenches both 30-40 cm deep and very similar in appearance. They contained the bones of two (possibly three) children, and one foetus or neonate. Amidst the sterile trenches was one oval depression, 40 x 30 cm, which contained the remains of an incomplete foetus (aged about seven months) and three beautifully-made racloirs. Another later (1921) find was of a gently sloping trench covered with stones which contained the well-preserved skeleton of a three-year-old child with the skull separate and upslope from the body. The skull was covered with a triangular limestone slab with a cup-shaped impression on the underside. The reason for the separation of the head is unknown, the activities of predators have been suggested and this seems likely. Further inside the shelter, and in a very disturbed zone, were cranial fragments, vertebrae, and ribs of a child aged about two. All the graves are located at the bottom of the lowest Mousterian layer, and are associated with tools of the Ferrassie Mousterian. The preservation of the bones is variable and many of the skeletons are very young and thus very friable. The two adults were buried in the front of the cave but the young children and foetus in the centre. One of the children's graves had a circular domed mound heaped over it, and another eight (sterile) mounds were found placed in rows of three. It is interesting that almost every

Neanderthal buried in western Europe is associated with the Quina-Ferrassie Mousterian and none with Denticulate or Typical industries (p.40). This might suggest that only one group of Neanderthals habitually buried their dead and the others were more casual, perhaps exposing them on platforms outside the cave, placing them in trees, cremating them or eating them.

It is incontestable that the majority of Neanderthal remains have been found in cave sites, but this is presumably because the deposits in caves and rock shelters have a better chance of preservation. Many open sites in north-east Europe (Germany, Poland and Russia) must have been obliterated during the last glaciation. Recent counts and other references make the totals given in Table 4.[7]

Table 4

Burial sites	No. of Neanderthals	Area
44	86	Europe
12	45	Near East
12	24	Elsewhere (not including sub-Saharan Africa)
68	155	

Two sites (Skuhl with ten skeletons and Shanidar with nine) have produced nearly half the Near Eastern quota, and recent finds from Djebel Qafzeh and Djebel Ighoud have not been included.

The two most important Russian burial sites (Kiik-Koba[8] and Starosel'e[9]) are both in the Crimea, one of the most thoroughly-excavated areas of Russia. The Crimean peninsula, some 27,000 square kilometres on the northern side of the Black Sea, may be divided into two broad geographical regions: the steppe area of the north, and the mountains of the south. The latter consists of three parallel ranges oriented approximately east-west, most of the archaeological sites being located in the second range which averages about 500 m in height and is cut by several small rivers leaving steep-sided limestone gorges honeycombed with caves.

Kiik-Koba cave is situated at the foot of one of these large limestone massifs, some 150 m above the river Zuya (Fig.22). Two distinct Mousterian complexes are present, the lower being basically a Denticulate Mousterian, though differing in many ways from the French Denticulate Mousterian, and the upper including many tools with a stepped retouch which is a particular feature of Quina Mousterian assemblages. The fauna includes three species of animals still present in the area today and the archaeological debris has features such as hearths and a possible storage pit which indicate intensive occupation. The importance of the site lies in the presence of a grave roughly rectangular in shape and dug into the decaying bedrock. The grave (oriented east-west) contained the burial of an adult Neanderthal but much of the skeleton has been removed by later disturbance. In the western end the bones of the right leg and both feet still occurred in anatomical order, together with other fragments of the skeleton. Bonch-Osmalovskii considered this skeleton to be more primitive than the general run of Neanderthals, a proposition discussed further on p.23. Some 30 cm north of the north-east corner of the adult grave was the skeleton of a one-year-old child, very badly preserved and never properly published.

The other site, Starosel'e, is located 12 m above the bottom of a dry ravine, and consists of a shelter composed of two recesses linked by a passageway some 8 m wide. The southern recess has a Mousterian industry, with a very high percentage of side scrapers, which resembles the Quina subdivision of the French Mousterian of Charentian facies. Bone tools were used as retouching implements and many of the faunal bones (which principally came from cold-loving animals such as reindeer and arctic fox) had scratches and tool marks from butchering. In the approximate centre of the southern recess the skeleton of a small child was found in association with animal bones as well as artefacts. The child seemed to be about eighteen to nineteen months old, but this is difficult to determine with any accuracy due to the lack of comparative Neanderthal material (comparisons have to be made with modern infants of the same age which may be misleading). Roginski found it to have some typical Neanderthal features as well as some distinctly modern characteristics and

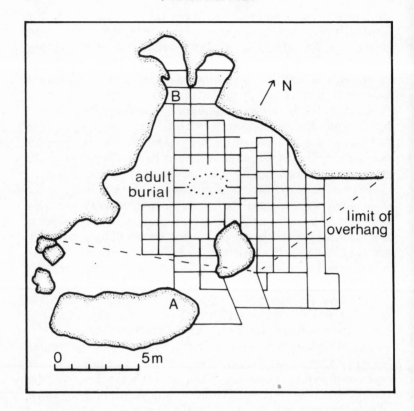

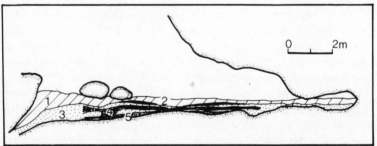

22. (a) Floor plan of Kiik-Koba cave (after Bonch-Osmalovskii)
(b) Section of Kiik-Koba deposits: 1. black level 2. compact brown layer under black 3. yellow *suglinok* 4. dark brown *suglinok* 5. dark basal *suglinok*.

Formozov emphasised the modern.[10] Klein[11] concludes that it is really impossible to assign it to either Neanderthal or *Homo sapiens sapiens* without comparative material. A reconstruction drawing of the child's appearance was made by the anatomist Gerasimov, whose work has already been discussed.[12]

There is no doubt that the Middle Palaeolithic sites of the Crimea date to the Würm, although an early paper by Gronov assigned them to the Riss.[13] It is, however, possible that the Crimean sequence begins as early as the Riss-Würm interglacial and sites such as Kiik-Koba may be early although there is no associated fauna to prove it. The industries are generally Denticulate Mousterian although some are Quina Charentian type, a subdivision which is not helpful for dating since such industries were made in different sets of ecological conditions in France. Industries of Charentian type are also found at Teshik-Tash (p.105) and Jabrud (p.121), and Klein considers it possible that the Charentian Mousterian represents a 'highly specialised technological response to environmental conditions'. The Mousterian inhabitants of the Crimea were exploiting two distinct environmental zones, the forested slopes of the Crimean mountains and the colder dry steppes to the north, and presumably used open air sites as well as rock shelters. There is ample evidence to suggest that they practiced intensive hunting specialisations preferring, for example, wild ass at Starosel'e and bison at Il'skaia.

The Iraqi site of Shanidar, excavated by Ralph Solecki, yielded one of the most important collections of Neanderthal remains. It is important not only for the famous 'flower burial', a graphic illustration of the humanity of Neanderthal man, but also for the excellence of the excavation, correlating palaeoenvironmental observations with archaeology. Technologically the stratigraphy illustrates the extreme cultural conservatism of Mousterian industries in this remote area.[14]

The great Shanidar cave, only 600 miles east of Mount Carmel (p.121) is developed in Cretaceous dolomitic limestone in the Zagros mountains of northern Iraq. An intermittent stream flows at the foot of the slope to the west of the cave and stagnant pools remain there in summer. The present cave dwellers (Kurds) retrieve water in goatskin bags, a practice which probably echoes that of their forebears. The vast cave mouth is shaped like a broad triangle, the opening 24 m wide and 8 m high with an abrupt increase in height not far from the entrance towards a maximum of 53 m. Outside the cave a talus slope stretches down to the gully 43 m below. The Mousterian layers are 8.5 m thick and culturally stagnant, amazingly so bearing in mind that 2,000 generations could have flourished there during the 60,000 years of occupation. From bottom to top hardly any variation in the stone tool assemblage is found, with the exception of the transitory appearance of a basally-trimmed point. The Mousterian artefacts are culturally similar to those from Teshik-Tash in Uzbekistan (p.105) and the two sites are also similar in situation – mountain environments where the hunters concentrated on mountain goats. The Mousterian culture at Shanidar finished before that of the Levant. The upper part (layer D) of the Shanidar material is dated to 46,000 (Gr-2527) and 50,000 (Gr-1495), the younger of these two dates being on about the same level as Neanderthal (Fig.23). By projecting these dates backwards and estimating the amount of accumulated sediment Solecki calculates that the initial occupation of Shanidar must have been close to 100,000 BP, towards the beginning of Würm 1. In the Levant the youngest date for the Mousterian is 33,350 BP (Kebareh Cave, Israel) but in the Zagros Neanderthal man had been replaced by *Homo sapiens* by that time, probably by 35,000 BP. The Mousterian industries of Shanidar finished by 46,000 BP and are nearest to the French Typical Mousterian variant which Bordes considers ended much later in France, at about 38,000 BP.[15] The Zagros mountains formed a cultural backwater when compared to the Levant or Europe, yet the dates for the end of the Mousterian, and for the arrival of the maker of Upper Palaeolithic industries are earlier here in south-west Asia than in Europe. It would seem that the Neanderthal variant present in the Zagros was extremely near to the 'classic' western European form and very culturally conservative. This, combined with problems of communication, could mean that he became extinct here earlier than in

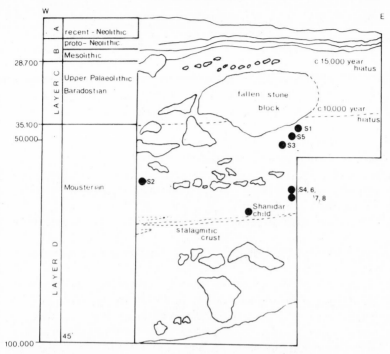

23. Section through the deposits at Shanidar (after Solecki).

Europe. Despite marked climatic fluctuations during the
occupation of Shanidar the tool kit remains essentially
unchanged, and the skulls of Neanderthals separated in time
by 15,000 years (Shanidar 1 who lived during a period of
warm climate and Shanidar 2 when it was much cooler) are
very similar. The postcranial skeleton of the Shanidar
Neanderthals is very like *Homo sapiens sapiens* in structure, and
possibly represents an interbred population living in a 'refuge'
area which did not mix culturally with other Levantine
groups. This isolation is, strangely, being repeated today in
the Kurdish tribes of the area which have recently been the
subject of great political controversy.

The adult Neanderthal Shanidar 1 (Fig.23) had been sealed
in an occupation stratum between two separate rockfalls, the
second fall (which killed him) occurring less than 100 years

after the first. The calvarium (brain-case) of the skeleton was much crushed on the rear of the top and left side of the head, the nasal bones also being crushed and the rest friable but well preserved. It was clear that the crushing happened before and not after death, due to the position of the head. The postcranial skeleton, associated with fragmentary mammal bones, charcoal flakes, flints and occupation debris, had also been crushed and broken by the rocks. Stewart considers it to be that of a male with an underdeveloped right shoulder blade (p.112) collar bone and upper right arm bone. The man, who had been crippled with a useless right arm, which had been amputated in life just above the elbow,[16] had been killed by the rockfall while standing on the sloping floor of the cave. The fall which struck him was a minor part of a large ceiling collapse which occurred towards the front of the cave, the body not being completely covered with stones since the softer soil bed on which he had been standing had absorbed much of the weight. He was old, perhaps forty in Neanderthal years, which might be the equivalent of eighty today, and suffered from arthritis. He was also blind in the left eye, as is indicated by bone scar tissue on the left side of the face. It is obvious that such a cripple must have been extensively helped by his companions, and had probably remained in the cave near the hearths while they went out hunting. Extensive wear on the front teeth suggests that in lieu of his arm he used his jaws for grasping while manipulating with his good left arm and hand, and the fact that his family had both the will and the ability to support a technically useless member of the band says much for their highly-developed social sense. One wonders whether he was the repository of tribal lore. The recovery of the skeleton, and its shipping down to Baghdad, is told by Solecki in his book. The skeleton was removed in a block of plaster-of-paris and shipped by train, as a passenger. But the station master, although permitting the foot and skull packages to travel, drew the line at the heavy torso package which must, he said, be sent by freight. Horrified at this potential dispersal of the precious fossil the excavation team solved the problem by asking the station master how he would like to have his head and body separated on the way to his final resting place.

As a result all the packages went first-class as passengers.

The second Neanderthal (Shanidar 2) had also been caught and crushed in a rock fall which compressed the skull laterally and contorted the neck. The bones were much crushed but reasonably well preserved. At first only the skull was removed due to difficulty of excavation, but later in the season the postcranial skeleton was obtained, much disturbed by rodents. A small collection of stones had been put over the body and a fire lit, several stone points and the broken bones of a funeral feast remaining in the hearth, which had been quenched with soil while still burning.

Shanidar 3 was also the victim of an accident, and had, it seems, been sitting at home recovering from a spear wound (a rectangular wooden implement making a cut in the ribs) when he was trapped by the fall. The remains were much crushed and the head and arms not recovered. Shanidar 5 was another adult found less than 0.6 m from 3, again a death by rockfall with much post mortem displacement. At the time of death he had been in a crouched position with hands over knees and the lower limbs doubled up. A further series of remains included a complex of a male, two adult females and a baby, but it is the male Shanidar 4 skeleton which is of surpassing interest due to the associated ritual. Shanidar 4 was a relatively complete adult laid on his left side facing west, with its head to the south. The man had been buried in a grave hollowed out among the rocks and covered over with earth from the living floor of the cave. Detailed and precise pollen analysis of the grave soil and surrounding levels showed that the body had been laid to rest on a bed of brightly-coloured flowers, probably woven into wreaths with a pine-like shrub. Pollen analysis showed that Shanidar 4 had been buried sometime between late May and early July. The pollen of at least eight species was represented, mostly small brightly-coloured wild flowers, relatives of the modern grape-hyacinths, batchelor's buttons and groundsel, which had been woven into the branches of the pine-like shrub. Other (control) samples contained traces of windblown pollen but in the samples associated with 4 pollen from particular species occurred in clusters of tens and hundreds, which was no accident of nature or sample contamination. In addition some of the pollen grains seemed to be resting inside the anther (pollen-bearing part of the flower) suggesting that the flower itself had been present, not just the blown pollen. The following genera were represented:[17]

Compositae (daisy family)
  Achillea type
  Centaurea type (*C. solstitialis*, St Barnaby's thistle)
  Senecio type (groundsel)
Liliaceae
  Muscari type (grape hyacinth)
Gnetaceae
Malvaceae
  Althea sp. (hollyhock)
  Ephedra altissima

Pollen from two other species also occurred but could not be identified. The Compositae are the daisy family, and at least six species of the genus *Achillea* are found today in the Shanidar area, including yarrow or milfoil which is used in herbal medicines and for application to wounds. *Centaurea solstitialis* is also used for the same purpose as well as being eaten, and is a striking plant with white leaves and rounded heads of pale-yellow flowers. Of the groundsels *Senecio vernalis* occurs near the site and has big bright-yellow flowers. It is also used as a wound poultice. The species of *Ephedra* has flowers which are not so conspicuous but whose branches could be woven together to make a bed or wreaths. The hollyhock pollen occurred as isolated grains, not clusters, but was very abundant. Its roots, leaves and flowers make a whole range of medicines to relieve everything from toothache to spasms, and it has been described as the poor man's aspirin. It seems most unlikely that Neanderthal man was unaware of the medicinal properties of these plants and very possible that the charming idea of burying the dead with flowers was accompanied by some deeper motive, perhaps wishes for its re-birth by applying known remedies for sickness.

The pollen evidence suggests that Neanderthal man occupied Shanidar during alternating warm and cool episodes, although the coldest would not reach the low temperatures of the maximum glaciation of Würm 3, which caused their Upper Palaeolithic successors to abandon the site. The Neanderthals probably made a seasonal round of their hunting territory and returned to the cave in winter, although the burial of Shanidar 4 in early summer means that they must sometimes have been there at that season too. The animals hunted were not so variable as those which formed the diet of their Levantine neighbours who had a more varied local environment to draw on. They consisted of goats, sheep, wild cattle, pigs, land tortoise, and (more rarely) bear, fox, martens, and gerbils, the carnivores possibly being killed for their pelts. Most of the common food animals lived in herds and could be hunted by running off cliffs or trapping in blind canyons. Coon says that most isolated hunters need a territory of between one and three square miles, and in the Zagros the artefacts from Mousterian sites are rather uniform, indicating a uniform culture.[18] The Zagros sites cover an area roughly 350 x 40 miles, making a territory of 14,000 square miles. If out of this one were to grant only their own valley to the Shanidar Neanderthals then their hunting territory would approach the lower limit of Coon's figures. Birdsell calculates that hunters who depended on local resources in the Pleistocene would have numbered about twenty-five per group, which is reasonable for Shanidar and can be paralleled in Aboriginal and Bushman organisation today.

In the Zagros mountain no large cutting tools are found, with the exception of a few handaxes at Hazar Merd. This is due to a scarcity of good raw material and does not occur in the Levant due to the availability of large chert nodules. As a consequence of the poverty of good stone the Zagros sites do not use the Levallois technique. The Shanidar Mousterian layers are capped by a 3-4 m Upper Palaeolithic (Baradostian) layer which did not contain any human remains and is thought to date to 35,000-28,000 BP. They hunted the same animals (mainly goats) as their Neanderthal predecessors but had a new stone and wood-working technology. The cave area was abandoned at the time of the last great cold period (about 20,000 BP), presumably for milder climates, but re-occupied in the Mesolithic at 15,000 BP.

The position of the body varies, in Neanderthal burials, from an attitude of rest to being violently flexed. It has already been suggested that flexed burial might represent a desire to reproduce a foetal or sleeping position or else be simply an economy measure, but there is a possibility that the burials were made tightly bound with the intention of preventing the dead returning.

Much controversy still exists upon the nature and significance of all manifestations of ritual behaviour in Neanderthal man but some attempt at synthesis was made in a seminal paper by Sally Binford, in 1968. Her survey was carried out in order to measure the degree of geographical and temporal variability in the Mousterian, and in the Upper Palaeolithic, and also to examine the treatment of the dead with respect to age and sex.[19] All the examples chosen came from Europe and the Near East, since these areas have yielded almost all the well documented burials. Some problems arose on what precisely constitutes a burial, for example an early publication of the La Quina find[20] noted that an articulated skeleton had been found in the shelter, but according to the excavator[21] its owner was a drowned Neanderthal who had been washed into the site by chance. Binford rejected this hypothesis on the principal of Occam's razor. Some deliberate Neanderthal burials were excluded from the sample (Table 6) because of their excavation conditions. An example is the adult male from Le Moustier, who had been buried and re-buried several times for the benefit of visitors, thus disturbing both the skeleton and grave goods.[22] The controversial burial at Combe Capelle was also excluded, as there is some doubt whether it is Mousterian[23] or Aurignacian.[24]

'Burial' in the sample studied by Binford is taken to mean the presence of an excavated grave and/or the arrangement of the body, or parts of the body, in a way which seems to preclude natural agency. This definition includes deliberate mortuary treatment, but does not necessarily require the remains to be placed in a covered grave. Binford discusses thirteen locations with complete or partial skeletons and

Table 5. Comparison of western European and Near-Eastern Neanderthal mortuary treatment[25]

	W. Europe		N. East	
A. *Population age distribution of human remains*				
infant	1		2	
child	11		6	
adult	9		13	
aged	1		2	
B. *Treatment of body parts*	Body part count	No. of sites	Body part count	No. of sites
skulls	10	6	1	1
cranial fragments	6	2	2	1
maxillary fragments	1	1	1	1
mandibles	6	4	2	2
arms	1	1	1	1
hands	0	0	2	1
legs	0	0	9	4
feet	3	2	1	1
C. *Frequency of burial furniture*				
present		9		5
absent		3		15
D. *Types of burial furniture*				
animal parts		4		3
bone flakes		4		0
pebbles		2		0
flint tools		8		1
stone blades		3		4
E. *Location of human remains*				
habitation area		3		20
non-habitation area		8		0
no data		2		1
F. *Body position in burials*				
legs – fully-flexed		3		10
semi-flexed		4		2
extended		0		1
no data		3		1
arms – fully-flexed		5		2
semi-flexed		2		10
no data		3		2
head – right side		2		1
left side		4		4
base of skull		0		3
facing up		0		1
no data		5		5

Table 6. Comparison of Mousterian and Upper Palaeolithic burials[26]

	Mousterian	Upper Palaeolithic
A. *Frequency of single and multiple burials*		
multiple	1	8
single	34	16
B. *Population age distribution*		
infant	4	1
child	14	4
adolescent	0	10
adult	15	20
aged	4	9
no data	0	2
C. *Sex distribution*		
male	13	21
female	4	6
undeveloped	20	15
D. *Body position*		
legs – fully-flexed	13	14
semi-flexed	8	2
extended	0	11
no data	16	15
arms – fully-flexed	7	20
semi-flexed	11	1
extended	0	7
no data	19	13
E. *Frequency of burial furniture*		
present	14	24
absent	17	0
no data	4	0

seventeen sites with remains which occurred among the living debris, yielding a total of thirty-seven complete or partial Neanderthals in the thirteen burial sites, and at least thirty-nine additional individuals in living debris. Krapina with eleven to thirteen individuals (p.106) was not included since they were found in a fire layer throughly broken and charred, and have never been adequately reported. Examination of Table 5 shows that the treatment of the dead in western Europe differs from the Near East. If we assume that the

Neanderthal burials do not represent the total population but only those individuals singled out (for what reason?) for mortuary treatment, then the age figures show that the proportion of adults to children is almost two to one in the Near East but about equal in western Europe. In addition the western European child burials have a high frequency of children aged five to six (nine out of eleven children); strange as at this age the child has not yet reached puberty but has passed the age when infant mortality figures are at their highest. One can suppose either that children of this age were deliberately selected for burial or else that an inordinate number of children died at about this age, perhaps connected with the period after weaning (which would have gone on until the age of two or three in Neanderthals) when the child was away from its mother and more liable, for the first time, to the sort of accidents or mischance which would affect adults. The Near East and western Europe also differ in the kind of body parts which turn up on living sites. In western Europe twenty-three skulls or skull parts, excluding isolated teeth, appear in Mousterian debris and only four postcranial fragments. In the Near East there are six skull parts and thirteen postcranial fragments, nine of which are parts of legs. This suggests that body parts do not occur at random but were being treated differently in the two regions.

In both areas flexed burials are the rule but in Europe the legs are semi-flexed, whereas in the East they are more commonly fully-flexed (a state of affairs which also occurs in the Upper Palaeolithic). The treatment of arms in the two areas is the reverse. Grave goods are present in nine out of twelve cases in western Europe but rarer in the Near East, only five out of fifteen cases. In western Europe these tend to consist of flint tools, bone flakes covering the body, stone blocks on or around the remains, and pebbles of distinctive shape or colour. In both areas animal parts occur with similar frequencies in burials and in both areas males far outnumber females. In the Near East adults tend to be buried in the centre and towards the front of caves, while children tend to be placed to the rear or sides (an anthropomorphic factor, or pure convenience?). All the known burials in the Near East,

including the untabulated burials from Qafzeh, p.121, occur
within the living areas while the majority of those from
western Europe do not. As Binford pointed out, burial of the
dead in the centre of a living area involves the whole
residential group whereas burial in out-of-the-way caves
might just involve a smaller segment. There is, of course, no
reason to suppose that the dead were buried in their own
living area. Indeed it would be just as feasible to bury the dead
person in a neighbouring and temporarily empty cave rather
than disturb one's own accommodation, unless there was
some ritual reason for wanting the dead still associated with
the living. This might mean that the implements which occur
in the occupation levels into which the bodies are inserted are
not necessarily those of the group to which the dead man
belonged. Such an occurrence would invalidate many of the
conclusions drawn from the association of Neanderthal
burials with particular artefact traditions.

There is a much greater variation in body position in the
Upper Palaeolithic graves than in the Mousterian. All the
former also contain grave goods, sometimes very elaborate
ones, and abundant personal ornaments. This must be the
result of a series of complex cultural changes. Howell[27]
suggested that the morphological variability between the non-
classic (p.128) Neanderthal populations of the Near East, and
the 'classic' population of western Europe was very
significant, the latter being a small breeding isolate, with
distinct morphological differences from the generalised
('progressive') populations of the east as the result of genetic
drift. According to his theory it was the more 'generalised'
Neanderthals who were the major contributors to the gene
pool of modern man with the 'progressive' Neanderthals of
Skuhl and Qafzeh representing the transitional forms. The
differences in burial ritual between Near East and western
Europe support the idea of differences in population but do
not, of course, cast any further light on the genetic
background of the difference. In another paper Binford[28]
suggested that there was a series of basic adaptive changes in
the terminal Mousterian of the Near East which produced
new sub-species of man as well as new technological means of

coping with the environment. The structural similarities in the Near-Eastern Mousterian organisation in which increased status-differentiation (evidenced from richness and variety of grave goods) might have played an important role. However since Binford's work a series of further Neanderthal finds have been made in both areas as well as in Africa (p.115) and a fresh synthesis of mortuary treatment is probably required.

As we have already seen, the find of the grave of an old man in a Quina Mousterian occupation layer at La Chapelle (Corèze) was of vital importance in the growth of ideas about Neanderthal. Here the grave trench had been dug into the marly soil of the cave, its whitish fill in marked contrast to the archaeological layers. The trench was sub-rectangular in shape, 1.45 m long and 0.3 m deep, the burial oriented approximately east-west and the skeleton laid on its back with the head to the west, the left arm extended and the legs flexed to the right. This east-west orientation is interesting since it appears in several Neanderthal burials, for example that from Kiik-Koba (p.90). It would not be over-fanciful to suggest that there might be some connection between this orientation and the direction of the passage of the sun. Alongside the head of La Chapelle man were three or four pieces of long bone, together with the remains of the metatarsal of a large bovid, the first two phalanges, and one second phalange. The bones had probably been cooked before burial which suggests that they represented food for the dead on his journey. Many of the bones surrounding the burial are also burnt, as is the surrounding sediment. The original excavators (p.16) concluded that the site had been a sepulchre where people came to eat (numerous) funeral meals but not to live, since the cave was too low arched for comfortable living, and there was no waste from tool manufacture. Although there is no sign of bones being used as tools they had often been cut for their meat and smashed to extract the marrow. This association of hearths with Neanderthal burials has been observed at many sites (e.g. Spy, Shanidar, etc.). At the former fires had been lit over the bodies, a common feature of Neanderthal burials. This might represent a ritual element, such as the provision of warmth to counteract the chill of death, but it is more likely to be the remains of a funeral feast fire, lit while the 'last rites' were being carried out.

The burials from the site of Mugharet-es-Skuhl (Mt Carmel, Israel) are interesting for a number of reasons (p.121). Five males, two females and three children were found buried in shallow graves, all the bodies being tightly flexed so that the feet touched the buttocks. There was little suggestion of ceremony except in the case of one man aged about forty-five who held in his arms the jaw bone of a huge boar, presumably either a hunting trophy or the cause of his death. One of the corpses had also died as the result of a fatal spear wound, the point of a wooden implement had passed through the tip of the thigh bone and hip bone socket and ended up inside the pelvic cavity.

One very important burial site is the grave of a child at Teshik-Tash, a cave situated in a deep Jurassic limestone gorge in the south-western spur of the Gissar range, 125 km south of Samarkand (see Fig.19). The name means 'stone with an opening' and the cave, which was entirely excavated by a Russian team[29] is 1,500 m above sea level. The gorge is only 15-20 m wide at this point and has sheer vertical walls. The burial was found in the first cultural layer near the west wall (Fig.24) and the skull was much smashed by the weight of overlying deposits, ending in over 150 fragments. The bones of the skeleton were disarticulated and incompletely preserved. The skull probably originally lay parallel to the west wall with the feet towards the entrance; intentionally buried in a shallow grave pit excavated in the sterile stratum directly below archaeological layer 1. The occupation of the cave was restricted to an area of about fifty square metres in the central portion of the excavated deposits, towards the front of the cave but well within the chamber formed by the rock overhang, the rear portion of the chamber hardly being used at all. The skeleton was associated with five or six pairs of horns of the Siberian mountain goat *Capra siberica*, which had been arranged vertically in pairs with the pointed ends down, delimiting a circular area within which the skull and the other remaining bones were lying. All the horns were from large (adult) individuals. The skeleton was much disturbed,

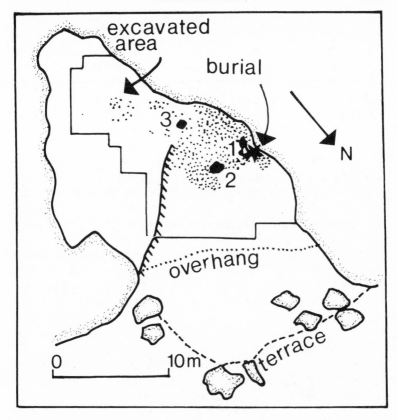

24. Floor plan of Teshik-Tash cave, showing the three hearths found in cultural layer 1 and the extent of the excavated area. The burial with goat horns was associated with hearth 1 (after Movius).

probably due to the attentions of the cave hyaena whose sharp teeth marks are visible on the ends of the long bones. A few animal bones, much broken, were associated with it, together with the coprolite of an unidentified carnivore. The child's humerus had the epiphyses missing, apparently gnawed off. 20 cm below the cranium there was a small block of limestone 21 x 18 cm in size, which seemed to have been inserted to support the block of material on which the head had been placed. A small hearth had been made alongside the horns, the base of one of the pairs of horns being slightly charred. However, the underlying clay was not reddened, and it seems likely that the fire only burnt for a very short time. Its relationship to the burial makes an association with some form of funerary ritual very probable.

The fact that so many of the Neanderthal burials were of children suggests that the destination of the bodies of dead children was of particular concern to them. In modern cases this is often associated with a belief in rebirth and return to life. The goat horns are also of interest since there is still a goat-horn cult in Asia today,[30] the survival of the pre-Islamic cult of Burkh (the mountain goat) which the cattle-raising people of the Khingove valley believe will bring them prosperity. This has its roots in an ancient hunting society, when life depended on the goat. Nowadays goat horns are collected only as ritual offerings, but once they belonged to the sanctuaries in very much the same way as the Copper-Age peoples of Anatolia accumulated bull horns. Such a cult definitely has its roots in extreme antiquity, possibly as far back as Neanderthal times, as is indicated by this burial.

There is evidence to suggest that cannibalism preceded the arrival of Neanderthal man. The site of Krapina, a rock shelter developed in sandstone overlooking a river in northern Yugoslavia, yielded in an 1899 excavation a series of fossil remains, probably representing between eleven and thirteen individuals with signs suggestive of cannibalism. Over 500 bones were recovered, many of them charred and some showing signs of having been cut. The fossils have never been adequately published and no living-floor patterns are available, due to the bad excavation. However if the bones, which occur mixed up in occupation debris, truly represent the remains of meals this would accord well with the widespread custom of ritual murder followed by consumption of the brain which is evidenced from several Neanderthal sites. The Krapina remains also include human long bones split lengthways, as for the extraction of marrow.[31]

Garn and Block[32] looked at cannibalism from the point of view of dietetics. The edible muscle mass of a 110 lb man yields only 10 lbs of useful protein even if he is skillfully butchered. Although the flesh is supposed to be nutritious and tasty its unit mass when compared with that of a bison is negligible. However in historical times hunger is rarely the reason for cannibalism and human flesh is eaten for ritual reasons. Bushmen, for example, consume the heart of a relative in order to acquire his strength. Modern society ordains that 'eating people is wrong' except in conditions of the utmost desperation (e.g. the recent Andean plane crash), and even then the taboo is so strong that people would sometimes rather starve than definitely risk social ostracism should their 'crime' be discovered. Murderers in primitive societies have been known to eat the flesh of the victim to prevent haunting by the ghost, and relatives of murdered men to aid them in the quest for revenge.

Ritual brain-eating occurs not only at Neanderthal sites but is also evidenced from fossil remains of a much earlier date, for example in fossils of *Homo erectus* and *Sinanthropus* (p.2). The Solo finds from Java occurred in gravel and sand deposits dating to at least 100,000 BP and comprised eleven skulls but no other skeletal parts, with the exception of two leg bones. Each skull had the facial bones smashed off and no jaws or teeth remained. The foramen magnum at the base of the skull had been opened in all but two of the Solo examples, by hacking with stone or wood tools. At least one of the owners of the skulls had been killed by crushing blows to the back of the head.

An even earlier 'murder' seems to have occurred in Germany. The Ehringsdorf skull is of particular interest, since it is an early Neanderthal (dating to the last interglacial at around 150,000-200,000 BP), although with many sapiens-like features, presumably a representative of the unspecialised hunters of Europe before the racial proliferation of the early Würm. The frontal area of the skull has clearly been hit by stone weapons, and there seems little doubt that its owner was murdered, the cranial base being opened to extract the brain.[33] The skull, in a very fragmentary condition, is that of a woman who had been killed by being repeatedly clubbed on the forehead before having her head severed from her body. The cranium was associated with the remains of a ten-year-old child and the jaw of an adult. Identical disfigurements occur today among the head hunters of Borneo and Melanesia where the object is to extract the brain and eat it. Among certain New Guinea tribes a child cannot be named until a man, whose name is known, has been killed and mutilated in this way. The father of the child extracts the brain, bakes it with sago and eats it[34] and after this the infant can bear the name of the dead man. The skull is kept as a sacred object until the death of the new bearer of the name.

At Monte Circeo, a limestone hill fifty miles south of Rome, a cave about 4.5 m above sea level was revealed while making extensions to the terrace of a seaside inn. It had been sealed off by a landslide in antiquity, probably in a late phase of Würm 1, 60,000-55,000 BP, and an inner chamber, where a shallow trench had been scooped out near the furthest wall, contained a single human skull surrounded by an oval ring of stones. The mutilated skull found at Monte Circeo was the remains of an old man who had been perhaps forty-five at the time of his death which was violent and possibly the result of actual murder. One mutilation, which was the result of blows to the right temporal region, caused damage to the frontal, temporal and zygona (cheek-bone),[35] and the second mutilation consisted of the careful opening of the foramen magnum (the hole through which the spinal cord enters the skull), in a manner identical to that already described from Solo and Ehringsdorf and also to the practices of modern head hunters in Melanesia. Among modern head hunters the most frequent way of dispatching the victim is to strike a blow with a heavy wooden axe on the temporal area of the head. In this case the victim must have been beheaded and the skull mutilated outside the cave, since there are no skull fragments inside. The skull rested on its forehead and left parietal, with the mutilated base upwards, rather as if it had been used as a cup. It is possible that some of the bones in other chambers of the cave could represent the remains of ritual offerings.

Similar mutilations occurred in the Ngandong remains found in 1931 in crania (p.135) of Neanderthal type. Eleven mutilated skulls and two tibias were associated with over 2,000 animal bones, representing every part of the skeleton.

All the skulls had the base mutilated in the same fashion, and Ngandong 5 had been murdered by strong blows on the occipital region in the same way as the man from Monte Circeo.

Blanc suspected that the Neanderthaloid Steinheim skull had also received similar mutilations. It is therefore incontestable that mutilation of the skull base was carried out both by early and late Neanderthals and Neanderthaloids for at least 250,000 years. Such mutilations do not systematically occur in the Upper Palaeolithic but are found again later in prehistory.

Ritual, or ceremonial, appears to have played an important part in the Neanderthal way of life, not only in connection with burial. The first appearance and use of symbolism which recurs throughout Upper Palaeolithic times, and again in later prehistory, being of especial interest. An example of this may be seen in what seems to have been a deer ceremony in a cave in the Lebanon,[36] where the Neanderthals had butchered a fallow deer, placed the meat on a bed of stones and sprinkled it with red ochre. The association of red ochre (haematite; iron oxide) is common in prehistoric burials since it seems to have appealed to early man as a blood-symbol.[37] Upper Palaeolithic burials associated with ochre are very common, and the use of the colour red in funerary ritual survives by custom even into the present day with the burial of a Pope in the traditional red shroud. We are, of course, uncertain of its meaning for early man, whether it was intended to bring life back to the corpse, represent the life that had gone out of it or merely act as decoration. Neanderthal man seems to have made use of the same pigment as a painting medium (p.51), a practice which was certainly continued by his successors.

At the Basua Cave 'Cave of Witches' in Savona a vaguely zoomorphic stalactite was employed by Neanderthal man, whose footprints still survive there, in some sort of ceremony which consisted of using it as a target for clay pellets.[38] This occurred in the interior of the cave, whose floor was rich in cave bear deposits, some 450 m from the opening – suggesting that the target practice was unlikely to be just a game which would surely have been carried out in the light. This is, perhaps, the first evidence of Neanderthal man using unmodified zoomorphic cave features in a ritual, which must be the precursor of the models, paintings and engravings of the succeeding Upper Palaeolithic, presumably serving the same purpose.

At Drachenloch, one of the bear-hunter sites in the Swiss Alps at an altitude of 2,440 m, the front part of the cave seems to have been occupied by Neanderthal man. Further back in the cave is the remains of a curious ritual connected in some way with the cult of the cave bear. A cubical chest of stones had been built, 1.03 m per side, the top covered by a massive stone slab. Inside this were the skulls of seven bears arranged with their muzzles facing the cave entrance, and still deeper in the cave a further six bear skulls in niches along the wall. Next to these skulls were bundles of limb bones, but the skull and the limbs frequently belonged to different bears. In one case a leg bone had been thrust through the arch of the cheek bone. The cave bear (*Ursus speleaus*) was very large (2.75 m tall) and extremely fierce, living in caves during the winter and hunted in the higher mountains during the rest of the year. At first it seems inconceivable that so much trouble would be taken over simple hunting trophies, although when one thinks of the walls of dead animal heads still seen in baronial fastnesses in the present day an explanation of the site as 'hunting magic' does not seem too far-fetched. Are we doing just the same thing? A similar cave bear cult is seen at the French site of Regourdou (Fig.3). Here a rectangular pit contained the remains of at least twenty bears and was covered by a massive slab weighing nearly a ton.

Bear rituals are performed by a number of hunting people in high latitudes, and certain Siberian tribes worship the bear as the mythical first man and apologise before killing it. Bears recur time and again in myth and legend. In Tibet the bear is held to be a sacred animal, and the Ainu hunters of Japan have an elaborate ritual involving the nursing and eventual sacrifice of a bear cub to ensure good hunting, the bear being seen as a messenger to the forest gods. Richard Adams in his elaborate fantasy *Shardik* creates a giant bear of supernatural significance and many cultures seem to envisage a special relationship between man and bear. The deceptively mild and friendly expression on the face of a bear has led to the legend that it is kindly disposed towards man; the human need for cuddly anthropomorphic objects creating the 'Teddy' bear which seems set to remain the most popular child's toy. Perhaps it is stretching one's imagination to connect a Neanderthal bear ritual of 50,000 years ago with Paddington and Pooh but nevertheless the bear seems always to have had a unique place in human mythology and to have been attributed a character and powers which it in fact never possessed.

The contribution of Neanderthal man to the visual and performing arts is speculative, but since these 'arts' were already developed at the time of Cro-Magnon man, shortly after 35,000 BP, it is not unlikely that they blossomed much earlier. Music, dancing and singing are possible but can never be proved, although a Russian excavator[39] has made a case for a 'mammoth bone orchestra' at the Upper Palaeolithic site of Mezin (p.58). The limited speech capacity of Neanderthal man must have made singing monotonous if not impossible, and had some simple instrument (a pipe or bone flute) been used it is surprising that none have been found. Visual art is another matter. Neanderthal man did not, it seems, favour personal jewellery although he may well have ornamented himself with paint. No Mousterian wall paintings are known yet lumps of red ochre are found inside hollow bones and reeds. Pieces of manganese ('crayons') show signs of having been rubbed onto a soft surface, are found at various sites. Perhaps they were used as body paint, mixed with water and grease before applying to the skin? The apparently fully-fledged art styles of the Upper Palaeolithic must have begun somewhere. A few ornaments are known. At Tata in Hungary there is an oval ivory fragment which has been polished and coated with red ochre, together with systematically scratched pebbles. At Pech de l'Aze a bone amulet was found, but the lack of perforated animal teeth is surprising since they are very common in hunting tribes. Perhaps the Neanderthal aesthetic sense was satisfied by the production of beautifully-made stone tools.

People have sometimes equated 'ritual' behaviour with a belief not only in the afterlife but also in some form of supernatural being (or beings) who have to be placated. This is probably not the case. A concern with the burial of the dead need not mean a belief in resurrection, it could be simply the manifestation of a tidy mind or a last expression of affection on the part of the bereaved. There is a very small number of Neanderthal burials when one thinks of the number of Neanderthals who must have died, and one may contrast this with our own culture where spiritual forces have affected social organisation to such an extent that it is illegal to leave a body unburied or uncremated. Yet Neanderthal man must have done so often, possibly exposing the dead in some way or making use of predators. We have no way of knowing why some Neanderthals chose to bury their dead, nor why they provided grave goods. All Neanderthal groups did not do so and yet the germ of the idea existed. Clearly Neanderthal men possessed such a very great diversity of behaviour patterns and codes of conduct that one cannot think of them as being one large ethnic group, rather a very diverse population who did not even look alike. Ritual has also been thought of as an attempt to control one's own destiny, which may often be the case. One interpretation of the cave-bear rituals could be the placation of the bears, or alternatively, ensuring success in hunting bears in the future.[40]

One must, however, admit that the Neanderthal concern with the quality of death (and presumably with the quality of life) marks a great evolutionary step forward. Care for the sick and old, as well as burial, implies concern for the individual, which might perhaps have arisen[41] as a response to particularly hard environmental conditions when people had greater need of one another than in times of relatively easy living. Perhaps the ties were more intimate, the mutual dependence of the extended families or hunting bands much closer. In our own times it is the people who are most depressed or very poor who have the highest hopes for a bright future in some other world. The Neanderthal brain was larger than that of previous species and capable, so it seems, of some degree of abstract thought. Questions must have been asked and answers arrived at. Ritual is, then, an attempt to reinforce the validity of the answers by expressing the belief that a connection exists between repetition and truth, if a possibility is repeated often enough it becomes a certainty. The greatest step forward taken by Neanderthal man is surely just this, the formulation of questions concerning abstract concepts and the development and transmission of the answers.

7

Survival or Extinction

One can say with certainty that the highly characteristic form
of *Homo sapiens* which we have called 'Neanderthal' has not so
far been found after the middle of the last Würm glaciation,
but this is about the only solid and incontestable fact
available. At present everything concerned with the
disappearance, 'extinction' or possible survival of the 'classic'
Neanderthals and the 'arrival' of *Homo sapiens sapiens* is highly
controversial, dozens of papers dealing with different theories
appearing every year. In the earliest days, after the finds of the
first Neanderthals, the situation was much simpler.
Neanderthal, being such a 'primitive' form, could not possibly
have been our ancestor and therefore must have been an
evolutionary sideline. He became extinct because, due to
interbreeding and cold-adaptation, he was unable to survive
in changing climatic conditions and was rapidly exterminated
by true progressive modern man who had evolved separately
in some (unspecified) part of the world and migrated into
western Europe. Apart from these questions there has also
been much speculation about the relationship between
Neanderthal and modern man. Did Neanderthal evolve into
Homo sapiens sapiens, and if so, what was the evolutionary
mechanism which accomplished such a change in so short a
time? Was Neanderthal man forced out of the best hunting
grounds and later exterminated by our ancestors because he
was at an evolutionary disadvantage due to problems with
communication or extreme cultural conservatism? How does
one account for the existence of forms which appear to be
'intermediate' or hybrids between Neanderthal and modern
man? Is this a result of interbreeding, or were the skeletons

representative of a population actively engaged in changing from one type of man to another? The stone tool industries themselves are a problem. Upper Palaeolithic layers were thought always to be separated from Mousterian layers by sterile deposits, but is it now known that this is far from being the case. Nor is it true that the latest Mousterian layers always show signs of technological deterioration; in many cases quite the reverse is true, and final Mousterian assemblages contain many implements (particularly those made on blades) which are characteristically Upper Palaeolithic. Even back in the days of the 'extinction' hypothesis it was suggested that relict populations of Neanderthals might have survived long after the death of their companions, eking out a miserable existence far from the best hunting grounds and eventually fading quietly away. And then there was the suggestion, at first dismissed as unquestionably 'lunatic fringe', that some of the stories told of creatures living in the high mountain regions of the Himalayas, Mongolia and the Caucasus might represent those relict-populations of Neanderthals who had retreated to a climate in which they were well fitted to survive, and where they were unlikely to meet with much competition. This suggestion is being taken very seriously by some extremely reputable scientists, and it is no longer possible to dismiss it out of hand. However, perhaps one of the most important discoveries which has revolutionised our thinking about the end of the Neanderthals is the discovery that relatively modern men (not *Homo sapiens sapiens* but indisputably not Neanderthal) were in existence long before the evolution of the latter. The old ideas of modern man evolving in some place in the east and migrating westwards around the 38,000-35,000 BP mark are no longer tenable. Populations of unspecific physical type were around well before 60,000 BP, a fact which was suspected after the discovery of the fossils from Kanjera in 1932, Fontéchevade in 1947 and Swanscombe in 1936, but has been confirmed by the new finds from the Omo valley, Djebel Qafzeh and La Chaise. These hominids lived in Africa and the Middle East as well as Europe and are associated either with undetermined flake industries (as at Omo), or with advanced Acheulean industries (La Chaise), or with a Mousterian industry with no Upper Palaeolithic component (Qafzeh). The most widely accepted and convincing view of the end of the classic Neanderthals is to envisage this unspecialised population, which existed in Europe during the late Riss and Riss/Würm, evolving along several different lines during the latter period, and during the early Würm. One of these lines led, by some as yet ill-defined mechanism, to a group of people with highly distinctive facial characteristics, which we have called 'Neanderthals'. Another line lead to modern man, who eventually replaced Neanderthal man in the archaeological record when some forms of the latter had become over-specialised. The so-called intermediate forms may indeed be the result of interbreeding but may also be the result of yet another racial 'line'. We have already discussed the suggestion that the late (classic) Neanderthal face could have evolved into modern man through such means as improved cultural sophistication. It is interesting to note that the Neanderthal fossils are much more diverse than the Upper Palaeolithic fossils, and modern skeletons are remarkably homogeneous. This would indicate that modern 'racial' differences are small and relatively recent acquisitions superimposed on a basic and modern norm. The early Neanderthal crania from Saccopastore, Ehringsdorf and Krapina C seem to be closer in form to modern man than the 'classic' Neanderthals, which would be expected since they would be closer in time to the original unspecialised population. We may therefore take as the best conclusion the idea that widespread (but varied) early Neanderthals developed from evolved *Homo erectus* populations in various areas, and from this stock later populations of *Homo sapiens* differentiated. The idea that anatomically modern man arrived very early, before Neanderthal, is not tenable. The early populations were unspecialised and then underwent local evolution.

It seems likely that the highly specialised Neanderthal groups played no part in the development of present-day man, who was, however, living at the same time. They probably kept their appearance and their culture and lived their conservative lives apart. The pace of evolution was probably determined by the relationship between the different groups of Neanderthals and non-Neanderthals living in the same areas. One could view an analogy of the situation as a flat surface covered with drops of water. If the table is tilted some of the drops come together and form new drops but some of the drops remain motionless due, perhaps, to some surface irregularity. Here the tilting is carried out by the effect of time and fluctuating climates in the late Middle and Late Pleistocene. The small drops of water are the mixed unspecialised populations of men living in the world at the time, and the drops which remain isolated are those which, for reasons of choice, geographic isolation or necessity (related perhaps to difficulty in communication) did not interbreed freely and tended to become morphologically extreme. This must be regarded as a continuing séance with the table still turning, the racial divisions which we see today being the latest results of a polycentric evolution, and the extreme Neanderthal forms of the past being some of the water drops which fell off the table and disappeared.

It is interesting to survey from an historical perspective the changing viewpoints about Neanderthal man's shape, distinctiveness and disappearance. Brace[1] was of the opinion that the (then) current view of Neanderthal as an aberrant and peculiar side branch which became extinct without descendants had its origin in the anti-evolutionary interpretations following the work of Boule in the early years of this century (p.16). The theoretical basis for this is the theory of catastrophism, which sees the fossil sequence as the result of a series of global catastrophies with their attendant extinctions and subsequent invasions. When this is applied to hominid fossils it becomes impossible to envisage the idea that hominids who differed in appearance from modern man could be ancestral to him. In his 1964 paper Brace recognised *Australopithecus* as the earliest ancestor of modern man (a concept which we have already seen needs much refining, p.2), and extended the original idea of an evolutionary tree from *Australopithecus – Pithecanthropus – Neanderthal – Homo sapiens*. He related this to advances in brain size which conferred a selective advantage, and saw the progressive reduction of the dentition (and therefore the entire facial skeleton to which it is related) as the answer to the problem of why the Neanderthal face changed into that of modern man (p.3).

Brothwell, commenting on this theory,[2] has pointed out just how poor the fossil record is. For the period between 250,000-80,000 BP there is hardly a scrap of human bone yet hundreds of generations and a billion corpses could have died. Can one ever say with certainty that only one hominid (or human) species exists or existed at the same time? We know that Neanderthal man and *Homo sapiens sapiens* overlapped to a certain degree and it is quite possible that we ourselves are overlapping with another hominid who has yet to be properly described but is notable chiefly for its large feet and elusiveness (p.129).

The question of the precise terminology for the less extreme Neanderthal populations of pre-Würm Europe is open to discussion. Some authorities call them pre-sapiens, and some even pre-Neanderthal. Brace suggested *Homo sapiens europensis* but this is not a good idea as it is giving too tight a definition to an amorphous group of hominids of which we know very little. Few people would now dispute the fact that there are marked physical distinctions between the 'classic' Neanderthals of western Europe and the Middle East and the less specialised forms present elsewhere. Howell[3] saw these physical distinctions as the result of a more open gene pool, which existed in eastern Europe and south-western Asia, influenced by environmental factors accentuated by periglacial conditions in the central European corridor, making movement difficult and encouraging interbreeding within the western European Neanderthal tribes. This view, discussed below in more detail, seems to underestimate the ability of Neanderthal man to adapt to different climatic conditions. Howells did not agree with the idea of a 'double line of evolution', but saw early populations of the same species (*Homo, sapiens neanderthalensis*) differing in taxonomically minor ways.

It is, of course, unfortunate that an example of the youngest and most extreme form of the Neanderthal stage was chosen as the type for Neanderthal man, but this was the first to be discovered. Brace postulates the theory that the Neanderthal face needed to be large to support the massive front teeth, which themselves were a technological advantage for use as a tool in holding the ends of material. This is supported by examination of many fossil teeth which bear evidence of wear patterns resulting from softening hides by chewing and from holding meat in the teeth to cut it. A big, thick jaw is needed to withstand such stress and the brow ridges function as an anchor for the muscles. The bunlike extension of the back of the Neanderthal skull would have balanced the out-thrust face, distributing the weight of the head evenly on its supporting point at the top of the spine.

Pilbeam[5] has suggested that the modernisation of the Neanderthal head is the result of changes in the vocal tract, as the upper part of the throat changed into a pharynx capable of producing the full human sound range. In the long low Neanderthal skull a shortening of the skull base (as a result of the evolution of the arched pharynx-roof) would have caused the facial area to pull inwards from its out-thrust position. With the face thus pulled in, the whole brain case would become higher (more modern in appearance) to contain the same amount of brain tissue. Thus he sees no reason why Neanderthal man could not have evolved into *Homo sapiens sapiens* although he puts forward no theory as to why such changes did not occur during the preceding thousands of years, since speech is such a valuable asset.

The theory that environmental change played a large part in the development and extinction of Neanderthal man has been discussed by many writers. It is indisputable that during the severe phases of the Würm the western Scandinavian and Alpine ice sheets came to within 300 miles of meeting in Germany, and it has been suggested that the Neanderthals trapped behind this periglacial corridor remained isolated from the rest of the world,[6] and developed the features which were considered to be a good adaptation to cold. A 'fine-meshed genetic screen' has been proposed, restricting east-west contacts. This seems unlikely as some of the earliest Upper Palaeolithic cultures in Europe were living in conditions at least as cold as those which Neanderthal man coped with, and it is quite possible that Neanderthals had developed aids such as snowshoes or skis (which have not survived in the archaeological record) to facilitate movement in the winter. During the summer thaw very little impediment to movement would be offered. The climate at the time has also been advanced as a cause of the rickets which beset Neanderthal, since the vitamin D needed to combat this disease may be obtained chiefly from sunlight and shellfish. The latter certainly played a very small part in the general Neanderthal diet. The theory of an 'ecological catastrophe' necessitates Neanderthal man being so inflexibly adapted to cold that he was unable to handle the warm spell which occurred in Europe between 38,000 and 28,000 BP, but 'classic' Neanderthals are found widely outside the cold of northern Europe and there is evidence to suggest that they had thrived during earlier warm spells since much skeletal evidence is associated with 'warm' faunas. However the work of Howell, who considered that the 'classic' Neanderthals of western Europe and the 'progressive' Neanderthals of the Near East were the result of climatic influence, and of Coon,[7] who equated facial features with survival in extreme cold, influenced scientific thought for some time.

Pfeiffer[8] also discusses the influence of climate on the life-style of Neanderthal man, suggesting that in warmer climates it would have been easier for him to come together in large-scale co-operative hunting, following animals over their familiar trails, whereas in cold regions there was a tendency to disperse into single family units. To kill animals efficiently large groups are required, as is shown earlier by the Spanish Acheulean sites of Torralba and Ambrona, and later by the Upper Palaeolithic French sites which are virtually tent-townships. Pfeiffer suggests that full-scale hunting of big game by Neanderthals originated in the rich lands along the coast of Israel, Lebanon, and Syria, where the wild cattle, fallow deer, and other herd animals grazed in the valleys rising from the coastal plains. Spring migrations would have been the rule, as grass was scarce then, and the animals needed to move to pasturelands on the plains, returning in autumn to higher meadows in the foothills. This would result in a high concentration of hunters along the migration trails, a circumstance which might account for the variety and richness of the Neanderthal remains from this area, since they occur in a region which would have provided the best conditions for breeding outside a small group. A further suggestion is that a shift to a drier climate (indicated by pollen analysis for the period 44,000-40,000 BP) might have stepped up the pace of evolution and the development of modern man. With the herds becoming larger, bigger bands of hunters were needed, the richest and deepest sites occurring where the vegetation and game would have been the most abundant, in the valleys and western slopes of the coastal ranges.

The rich cave sites of the Middle East have produced Neanderthal remains in plenty whose interpretation is still open to doubt. Some of the sites have Mousterian deposits up to 23 m in thickness. The large Djebel Qafzeh cave, situated on the narrowest part of a pass to the mountains of Lebanon about fifty miles from Haifa (see Fig.5), yielded five individuals in the 1930s which were 'transitional' in type, resembling the remains from Mount Carmel. New excavations at Qafzeh yielded three additional skeletons from the original layer 17, with a Mousterian industry using the Levallois technique. Most were found in the same sector, at the entrance to the cave. The crania are very different from the classic Neanderthals and more like *Homo sapiens*, despite the associated Mousterian industry. This suggests that the equation of Mousterian = Neanderthal must finally be discarded in sites where there is no firm proof. The presence of *Homo sapiens* at the beginning of the last glaciation suggests that his origins must lie in the Riss-Würm or even in the Riss, and that during that time a changing population evolved two distinct trends, an evolution completed by the beginning of the Würm. The Qafzeh remains are contemporary with the Neanderthals of Europe.

The Skuhl rock shelter is the easternmost of the three neighbouring Mount Carmel caves investigated by Garrod between 1929-34, the others being Tabun and El Wad. Skuhl, a Neanderthal cemetery, yielded ten individuals and assorted other remains. For twenty years after their discovery the Tabun and Skuhl remains were thought to be contemporary, both on archaeological and faunal grounds, and their mixture of archaic and modern characteristics gave rise to much confusion. At first the remains were taken as two distinct populations,[9] then a large variable population,[10] a view which was opposed by Stewart[11] who upheld the first theory. The holders of the single population idea advanced two theories to account for its variability: either that the population represented an admixture of Neanderthal and *Homo sapiens*, or an evolution from one to the other. Twenty years after the first finds, speculation has been resumed[12] on the contemporaneousness of Tabun and Skuhl and whether or not they do indeed belong to a single population. New data relative to this question was obtained from recent excavations at Tabun[13] which concern the proposed 'faunal break' between Tabun B and C, the interrelationships of the industries, and the stratigraphic position of the Tabun 1 burial. Ronen concludes that a stretch of 20,000-25,000 years may separate the Skuhl and Tabun remains, and that the Skuhl sequence lasts longer than has hitherto been supposed. The Skuhl human remains seem definitely to belong to a late phase of the Middle Palaeolithic and the probability of the existence of two populations is high, with the *sapiens*-types of Skuhl and Qafzeh on one hand and the Neanderthals of Tabun-Amud on the other, but much remains unclear, and further excavation and detailed metrical work on the skeletons is obviously needed.

Table 7. Relative chronology of the Mount Carmel sites

Tabun		*El Wad*		*Skuhl*	
		F	Upper Palaeolithic		
				B	Mousterian
B	Mousterian				
C	Mousterian				
.........erosion............... spring activity..............					
		G	Mousterian	C	Mousterian
D	Mousterian				
E	Yabrudian				
F	Acheulean			C	sandy

The other caves at Mount Carmel produced equally controversial remains. The Tabun cave yielded a skeleton with brow ridges much less massive than the 'classic' Neanderthals of Europe, on a skull of modern shape. In the Skuhl rock shelter the ten individuals had longer and straighter limbs than Neanderthal, smaller faces, more prominent chins and a general air of modernity. The front of the skull and the lower jaws are so modern that had they been found together or singly they would probably be classified as *Homo sapiens sapiens* yet the back of the skull, if recovered alone, would have qualified as Neanderthal. Either these Middle Eastern finds are the result of admixture, or they are an unstable group with a wide range of variation from which *Homo sapiens* could have emerged. The third possibility, that they represent the remains of the old unspecialised forms of man, would be the most convincing, were it not for the dates and associated industries.

A Japanese expedition which worked at the cave of Amud, on the north-west coast of the Lake of Tiberias, produced four 'Neanderthaloids'. The cave, developed in Eocene limestone, seems to have filled during an interstadial between the early and middle Würm, but correlations from the fauna are at variance with the radiocarbon dates. The inhabitants of the cave seem to have hunted gazelle and fallow deer almost exclusively, and to have resembled the Neanderthals from western Asia in appearance, especially the ones from Tabun and Shanidar. Yet the Tabun B, C and D skeletons are dated to 39,700 ± 800 (GrN 2534), 40,900 ± 1,000 (GrN 2729) and 35,400 ± 900 (GrN 2170) while the dates from below the Amud man are less than 11,000 BP[15] due to contamination by modern carbon. The mammalian remains correlate with other sites and with a dry phase probably equivalent to Würm 1/2 interstadial, and the tools show a marked admixture of Levallois-Mousterian and Upper Palaeolithic tool forms but no evidence of separate industries. The proportion of Upper Palaeolithic forms such as end scrapers and burins to Middle Palaeolithic elements (retouched points, racloirs) is very high, and the industry appears transitional between the Middle and Upper Palaeolithic industries of the region.

The skull of the Amud man was very compressed and had a cranial capacity of 1740 cc (similar to the 'classic' Neanderthals of Europe). He was rather short (157.8 cm), like Shanidar and Mount Carmel, with a higher cranial vault than the classic Neanderthals, and a brow form very similar to Skuhl and modern in appearance. The excavator concludes that the Shanidar 1, Tabun 1 and Amud 1 finds have many characteristics in common, and probably represent a group of local Neanderthal variants who had a close racial affinity among themselves. He suggests that the plan shown in Table 8 might be feasible.

Table 8

Stage I	*Stage II*	*Stage III*	*Stage IV*
Shanidar 1	Amud 2	Skuhl 4	UP man e.g. C/M
Galilee Tabun I	Qafzeh 4		
Teshik-Tash			

Amud man is a variety of local Neanderthal bearing a racial affinity to the Tabun-Shanidar group and the Skuhl-Qafzeh group, and lying morphologically between them. One causative factor in the evolution of the face might have been the reduction of the upper and lower jaws, due to the weakening of the chewing muscles. Suzuki discusses the role of the chewing apparatus as a contributory factor, citing an example of facial changes in certain Japanese aristocrats over the past 250 years.[17] The Tokugawe Shogunate family (seventh–mid-nineteenth century) had their origins in the common people, but assumed political supremacy over Japan and quickly developed distinctive facial characteristics such as reduced lower and upper jaws, a lack of surface abrasion on their teeth and very poorly developed chewing muscles. This was a direct result of the 'easy life', eating soft, well-cooked food, which required no chewing action, and its effect was enhanced by selective mating. It is possible (but improbable) that technological or behavioural changes in Neanderthal man reduced the need for a robust heavy jaw and large chewing muscles. The 'classic' type of Neanderthal face would be transformed to a modern face through transitional stages such as Skuhl, the rate of change being especially noticeable in the Skuhl fossils where there are variations in the reduction of both lower and upper jaws.

One conclusion seems obvious, that the 'mass extinction' theory involving the systematic annihilation of under-privileged Neanderthals by incoming sapiens is simply not true. As Genoves pointed out there is no archaeological reason for such an occurrence although within the field of palaeontology mass extinctions are regular occurrences, frequently by unknown mechanisms, meaning that catastrophism still exists in biology. It has been said that it is 'doubtful that the capacity for systematic extermination arrived so early', but there are many historical and sub-contemporary replacements or very severe displacements of one human population by another without involving actual annihilation (American Indians, Highland Clearances, Aborigines). Some clarification of this point, and its chronological implications, may be gathered from a study of the stone tool industries.

Industries which could be called Upper Palaeolithic appear in north Africa and central Europe before 38,000 BP, and definite Upper Palaeolithic industries such as the Lower Périgordian before 35,000 BC. At Jabrud a pre-Aurignacian assemblage probably dates towards the end of Würm 2 (45,000-38,000 BP), suggesting co-existence of modern man, Neanderthal man and Mousterian industries with Upper Palaeolithic industries. Thus during this period there is no direct correlation between a particular human type and a particular industry. It would seem that the transition from Middle Palaeolithic (Mousterian) industries to Upper Palaeolithic industries happened in several places at the same time, and we must envisage Neanderthal either adopting new tool forms, borrowing those of his neighbours or being replaced by the makers of the Upper Palaeolithic industries who were better equipped to occupy the best hunting grounds. In western Europe, as we have seen, certain types of

Mousterian (Quina, Ferrassie, Typical, Denticulate) are definitely associated with Neanderthal, with no evidence of Upper Palaeolithic tendencies, yet we do not know who made the MAT (although it was probably Neanderthal), which was directly ancestral to the Lower Périgordian. It might equally well have been modern man or another variant which had evolved from the general unspecialised stock. It has been suggested that some of the Upper Palaeolithic industries which are very short-lived (e.g. the Szeletian) were the result of 'acculturation' on Neanderthals. The Aurignacian, which is totally unlike the Périgordian, was almost certainly imported into Europe by modern Cro-Magnon man, possibly from eastern Europe, whereas the Périgordian itself seems to have developed locally. The passage from Mousterian to Périgordian is fascinating but frustrating at the same time, due to the paucity of associated human remains. As we have already discussed, hybrid industries do occur, but their makers are unknown. In the upper horizons of sites like the Grotte à Melon[19] the fine Mousterian tools become increasingly rare, while the number of large coarse tools grows, giving the impression of a degenerate Mousterian. But most of the time the final Mousterian layers show industries which include large quantities of Upper Palaeolithic forms. An example of this may be seen at Jabrud,[20] where layer 15 lies between two Mousterian horizons, yet seems to be Upper Palaeolithic. Yet all the tools seen there are found abundantly in the evolved Mousterian. The same situation occurs at Kara Kamar (Afghanistan), and at Arcy-sur-Cure (p.57) a post-Mousterian layer has been found which seems to have been formed after the Würm 2/3 interstadial. Late Mousterian layers at Baume-Bonne occur during Würm 3, which must be contemporary with the Upper Palaeolithic Périgordian layers, which were being deposited at the same time in other areas. Peyrony[21] argued that Cro-Magnon man came into Périgord driving the makers of the Mousterian into Charente and Poitou where they might have remained until the coming of the Aurignacians, which could explain why the late Mousterian is so well represented in the northern Périgordian.

The Grottes d'Arcy at Arcy-sur-Cure (Yonne) are the

nearest cave sites to Paris, situated some 200 km to the south
east. Nine caves have been investigated, all cut into a massif of
Jurassic limestone and all having a southerly exposure. New
evidence from the Grotte du Reine shows conclusively that
long overlaps occurred between Mousterian and Upper
Palaeolithic occupations of the site, a fact of considerable
archaeological importance. Movius[22] suggests that in the final
Mousterian the technology for the production of flakes is
essentially Mousterian while the forms and variety of the tools
tend towards a new method of producing blanks. The
appearance of fairly numerous true blades in the upper
portion of the final Mousterian horizon together with the
presence of leaf-shaped points foreshadows the Upper
Palaeolithic. In other words, without losing its Mousterian
aspect the stone tool assemblage is beginning to look
typologically like the overlying Châtelperronian (Lower
Périgordian), the earliest Upper Palaeolithic in western
Europe. This period, which is neither true Mousterian nor
true Upper Palaeolithic, is characterised by the persistence of
flake production using the Levallois technique, the gradual
elongation of certain flakes to make true blades and
flake/blades, the development of tools whose function is
believed to have been similar to, if not identical with, those
characteristic of the earliest Upper Palaeolithic. At the Grotte
du Reine, discovered in 1949 by Leroi-Gourhan, there is
considerable evidence for climatic oscillation in the final
Mousterian levels which may be correlated with the known
climatic variations, the coldest episode being in layer 8
(31,550 ± 400 GRO 1736) (31,690 ± 250 GRO 1742). It
would appear from this site that the earliest Upper
Palaeolithic arrivals in Europe flourished during a cold
interval. The archaeological material from the final
Mousterian here includes such Upper Palaeolithic forms as a
carefully-polished awl made on a thick splinter of a long
bone,[23] and a series of curved natural-backed flakes which are
more or less identical with specimens from the
Châtelperronian of overlying levels.

Speaking in general terms it seems most advisable to view
the change in tool-making traditions as an evolutionary

process, the gradual replacement of one tradition by another, with many intermediate industries. Clearly this would not happen everywhere at the same time, and there will be sites where intermediate industries are missing, but it is the identities of the makers of the tools which present the greatest problem. In view of the fact that the Aurignacian is so definitely an imported culture and the Périgordian so obviously an evolution from one variant of the Mousterian it is difficult to see why different Mousterian traditions could not have been made by different types of man. Eventually, because one species (the 'classic' Neanderthals) seems to have become extinct, their tool-making traditions were taken over, modified, and extended by the less extreme forms, as well as various races of modern man.

On balance the evidence points to the gradual extinction of the 'classic' Neanderthals from the archaeological record and the rise to supremacy of anatomically modern man. The cause of this process is not fully understood but seems likely to have been extremely complex. There remains yet one possibility to be considered – whether or not it is feasible that relict Neanderthals might still exist; whether, indeed, the accounts of large hairy primates living above the snow line and called by a variety of different names might actually refer to Neanderthal. Looking at this logically there seems no reason why it should be impossible. It is unlikely that even the most extreme Neanderthals became extinct overnight, but rather that they were gradually replaced. Should this be the case then it would be natural for them to retreat to areas whose remoteness would make it unlikely that they would be discovered, and where they might have survived for 40,000 years or so, far less time than the duration of the period in which they occupied Europe. However there are many arguments against this theory and the legion of doubters who oppose anything remotely connected with 'Yetis' or their fellows is indeed numerous. It is advocated, with some truth, that no argument can be conclusive until positive skeletal evidence is produced. Others say that no large primate could survive in such a difficult climate, as its body mass would be so great that the necessary amount of food would not be forthcoming. However this theory relates only to the supposed inhabitants of the high Himalayas and creatures living in other areas such as the Almas of Mongolia and Sasquatch of the United States (Fig.25) would surely be able to obtain an adequate food supply. The amount of scientific interest in such creatures (which Napier groups under the general name of 'Bigfoot') is steadily growing; reputable scientific foundations in eastern and western Europe and America have given research grants and a large body of literature, photographs, footprint casts and ciné film is now available for study.[24] Russian projects have used modern market-research techniques to study the veracity of local legends, parties of scientists have spent many hours questioning Sherpas and in parts of America and Nepal killing a Sasquatch or a Yeti is a criminal offence. Our attitude towards Bigfoot is almost the same as the attitude of our grandfathers to Neanderthal, symptomatic of public reluctance to believe in anything unfamiliar. 'Bigfoot' is geographically widely distributed (Fig.25), and the reason for the name very obvious. The various accounts have been analysed and processed by Professor John Napier, the distinguished anthropologist and anatomist, whose book on the subject presents a scholarly biography of a series of most elusive creatures.[25] In common with Napier I believe that the evidence for the existence of the Yeti (Abominable Snowman) is unconvincing, and it is extremely unlikely that even if it does exist it would be related in any way to the subject of this book. In America the body of evidence for the Sasquatch is so convincing that it seems impossible that it does *not* exist, and even likely that several different varieties are alive in remote areas of California and British Columbia. But it is in Mongolia that a group of Yeti-like creatures called Almas are found, who seem to be of the greatest importance since all evidence points to their humanity and I, personally, feel that it is by far from impossible that they represent relict Neanderthals.

One of the questions that needs to be asked is whether it is possible to search for a large animal for a period of years and not capture or kill a single specimen. One could quote the example of the Giant Panda which was hunted in western

25. Location of 'Bigfoot' reports.

Szechwan (China) on the Tibet border for seventy years before one was collected alive. We have been hunting Bigfoot for much less time. Sanderson[24] makes the point that man must believe in something before he finds it, quoting examples of sites of the Folsom culture in north Mexico which had been seen for many years, but were not recognised until the antiquity of man in North America was generally accepted. But to return to the Almas. Reputable witnesses are involved and many of the reports are lodged in Russia, a country whose scientists are not renowned for their naivety. In 1905-7 one B. Baraidin, a specialist in eastern folklore, was commissioned to travel through Mongolia to Tibet on an assignment from the Russian Geographical Society of (then) St Petersburg. While doing so he encountered an Alma. On his return a full report was made but the head of the geographical society told him to delete it as 'no one will ever believe that, and it may prove embarrassing'. This is an attitude which is often found in Bigfoot stories. However since that time much work has been done in the area and there seems little doubt that such creatures do exist there. The precise region is called Dzungaria, an immense lowland pocket into which the steppes penetrate via two great valleys separated by the Tarbagati mountains. Professor Khaklov notes that the Alma distribution extends north to the Grand Altai and beyond that to the Sanyan mountains. The creature's footprints exactly match those of Neanderthal man discovered in a cave in Italy (Fig.26) and would seem to be a mountain-dwelling species since no reports have been received either from the lowlands or from the montane plateau. The creatures are small, rather hirsute and without speech understandable to the local inhabitants, who regard them simply as primitive humans. They have distinctively human traits and 'trade' with the local tribesmen by leaving skins at appointed places and taking away the articles left there. Professor Rinchen of the university of Ulan Bator quotes a story of a scholar in a Mongolian monastery who is a half-bred Alma (suggesting that the creatures are genetically related to us). Neanderthal, as we know, had a large brain but we are unsure of his intellectual capacities although these might have been considerable.

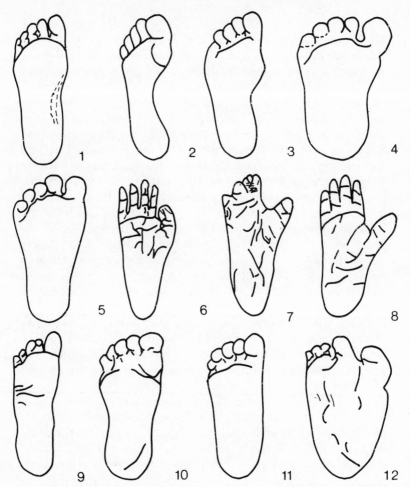

26. Footprints (after Sanderson): 1. Human adult – west Caucasoid, impression in clay mould 2. Human adolescent – west Caucasoid, age 14½, impression of left foot on hard surface 3. Cro-Magnon man – impression from clay floor in French cave 4. Neanderthal – from clay floor at Toirano, Italy 5. Bigfoot – from sketch of track in mud, Kirghiz, Russia 6. Monkey – old male rhesus, drawn from live specimen 7. Lowland Gorilla – photograph of cast 8. Chimpanzee – outline of extended foot from plaster cast 9. Human adult – Bushman, sketch made from a cast 10. Bigfoot – Sasquatch, from tracing of deep firm print in wet clay 11. Bigfoot – central Asian variant,.sketch from print 12. Bigfoot – Yeti, from Shipton's print.

Arguments in favour of accepting the possibility of Almas as hominids or relict Neanderthals are too numerous to be discarded without due consideration. One might stress, for example, that the area in question is very rich in Mousterian artefacts. There are also numerous stories concerning the relationships of the Almas to their sapient neighbours, with whom they appear to be on friendly terms.

At first sight the suggestion seems bizarre but could it be that Neanderthal is alive and well and living in Outer Mongolia?

Notes

1. Evolution and Neanderthal Man

1. M.H. Day, *Fossil Man*, London 1969.
2. D.S. Brose and M.H. Wolpoff, 'Early Upper Palaeolithic man and late Middle Palaeolithic tools', *American Anthropologist*, 1971, 73, 1156-94. C.S. Coon, *The Origin of Races*, London 1963. S. Sergi, *The Neanderthal Palaeoanthropi in Italy*, 1958, reprinted in *Ideas on Human Evolution* ed. W. Howells, Cambridge, Mass. 1962. A.J. Steegman Jr., 'Cold response body form and craniofacial shape in two racial groups of Hawaii', *American Journal of Physical Anthropology*, 1972, 37, 193-222.
3. H.V. Vallois and B. Vandermeersch, 'Le crâne moustérien de Qafzeh (Homo VI): étude anthropologique', *L'Anthropologie*, 1972, 76, 71-96.
4. F.M. Bergounioux, '"Spiritualité" de l'homme de Néanderthal', in *Hundert Jahre Neanderthaler*, ed. G.H.R. von Koenigswald, Köln-Graz 1958, pp. 151-67.
5. F.E. Zeuner, *The Pleistocene Period*, London 1959. R.G. West, *Pleistocene Geology and Biology*, London 1968. K.W. Butzer, *Environment and Archaeology*, London 1964. F.W. Shotton *et al.*, *Recent Advances in British Quaternary Studies*, Oxford 1977.
6. Shotton *et al.*, 1977, op. cit.
7. West, 1968, op. cit.
8. R.E. Leakey and R. Lewin, *Origins*, London 1977.
9. Ibid.
10. H. de Lumley and M.A. de Lumley, 'Découverte de restes humaines anté-néanderthaliens datés au debut du Riss a la Cauna de l'Arago (Tautavel, Pyrénées-Orientales), *Comptes Rendus Hebdomadaires des Séances de l'Academie des Sciences*, 1971, D. 272, 1739-42.
11. M.A. de Lumley, *Ante-Neanderthals and Neanderthals of the Western European Mediterranean Basin*, Paris 1976.
12. H.V. Vallois, 'La grotte de Fontéchevade 2° partie: anthropologie', *Archives de L'Institut du Paléontologie Humaine*, 29, 8.
13. G. Bohm-Blancke, *Altsteinzeitliche Rastplätze im Travertingebeit von Taubach, Weimar, Ehringsdorf*, 1960, Weimar: Alt-Thuringen IV, 151-200.
14. C.B. Stringer, 'Population relationships of late Pleistocene hominids: a multivariate study of available crania', *Journal of Archaeological Science*, 1974, 1, 317-42.
15. M. Boule, 'Les hommes fossiles', *Eléments de Paléontologie Humaine*, Paris 1923. A. Keith, *The Antiquity of Man*, London 1925. H.V. Vallois, 'Neanderthals and praesapiens', *Journal of the Royal Anthropological Institute*, 1954, 84, 111-30. G. Herberer, 'The descent of man and the present fossil record', *Cold Spring Harbour Symposium on Quantitative Biology*, 24, 235-44.
16. L.S.B. Leakey, *Adam's Ancestors*, London 1953. L.S.B. Leakey, '*Homo sapiens* in the Middle Pleistocene and the evidence of *Homo sapiens* evolution', in *Origin of Homo sapiens* ed. F. Bordes, Unesco, Paris 1972.

17. Ibid.

18. S. Sergi, 'Morphological position of the "Prophaneroanthropi"': Swanscombe and Fontéchevade', 1953, reprinted in *Ideas on Human Evolution*, ed. Howells. F.C. Howell, 'The evolutionary significance of variations and varieties of Neanderthal man', *Quarterly Review of Biology*, 1957, 32, 330-47. E. Breitinger, 'On the phyletic evolution of *Homo sapiens*', in *Ideas on Human Evolution*, ed. Howells. W.E. le Gros Clark, *The Fossil Evidence for Human Evolution*, Chicago 1966.

19. G. Schwalbe, *Die Vorgeschichte der Menschen*, Braunschweig 1904. A. Hrdlička, 'The Neanderthal phase of man', *Journal of the Royal Anthropological Institute*, 1927, 57, 249-74. A. Hrdlička, *The Skeletal Remains of Early Man*, *Smithsonian Miscellaneous Collections*, New York 1930, 83, p.1-379. F. Weidenreich, 'The Neanderthal man and the ancestors of *Homo sapiens*', *American Anthropologist*, 1943, 45(1), 39-48. F. Weidenreich, 'The palaeolithic child from Teshik-Tash cave in Uzbekistan', *American Journal of Physical Anthropology*, 1945, NS. 3, 151-62.

20. Coon, 1963, op. cit. C.L. Brace, 'The fate of the "classic" Neanderthals: a consideration of hominid catastrophism', *Current Anthropology*, 1964, 5(1), 3-43. Brose and Wolpoff in *American Anthropologist*, 1971, 73.

21. Coon, 1963, op. cit. Weidenreich 1943, op. cit.

22. F. Bordes, *The Old Stone Age*, London and New York 1968.

23. J.S. Weiner, 'The pattern of evolutionary development of the genus *Homo*', 1958, reprinted in *Ideas on Human Evolution*, ed. Howells.

24. D.R. Brothwell, 'Upper Pleistocene human skull from Niah caves', *Sarawak Museums Journal*, 1960, 9, 323-49. J.M. Bowler, A.G. Thorne and H.A. Polach, 'Pleistocene man in Australia: age and significance of the Mungo skeleton', *Nature*, 1972, 240, 48-50.

25. Lumley, 1976, op. cit. W. Howells, *Mankind in the Making*, New York 1959. F.C. Howell, *Early Man*, New York 1965. R.J. Braidwood, *Prehistoric Men*, Glenview, Ill. 1967, 7th ed. C.L. Brace, H. Nelson and N. Korn, *Atlas of Fossil Man*, New York 1971.

2. Appearance and Reality

1. K.P. Oakley, *Frameworks for Dating Fossil Man*, London 1964.

2. G.H.R. von Koenigswald, *Neanderthal Centenary*, Köln-Graz 1958.

3. M. de Puydt and M. Lohest, 'L'homme contemporaire du Mammouth à Spy', Mémoire Congrès Archaeologique, Namur, 1886, *Annales de la Fédération d'Archéologie et d'Histoire de Belgique*, 1887, 2, 207-40.

4. K.P. Oakley, B.G. Campbell and T.I. Molleson, *Catalogue of Fossil Hominids*, Publication of the Trustees of the British Museum (Natural History), London 1971.

5. J. Roche, 'La découverte de la Chapelle-aux-Saints et son influence dans l'evolution des idées concernant le psychisme des Néanderthaliens', *Les Sepultures Néanderthaliennes*, ed. B. Vandermeersch, 1976, IX Congrès UISPP Nice, pp. 14-23.

6. M. Boule, 'L'homme fossile de la Chapelle-aux-Saints (Corrèze)', *L'Anthropologie* 1909, XX, 519-25, 8 fig. M. Boule, 'L'homme fossile de la Chapelle-aux-Saints', *Annales de Paléontologie* 1911-13, VI, 115-72; VII, 102-208; VIII, 209-78. M. Boule and R. Anthony, 'L'encéphale de l'homme fossile de la Chapelle-aux-Saints', *L'Anthropologie*, 1911, XXII, 129-96.

7. W.L. Strauss and A.J.E. Cave, 'Pathology and the posture of Neanderthal man', *Quarterly Review of Biology*, December 1957.

8. D. Brothwell, 'Adaptive growth rate changes as a possible explanation of the distinctiveness of the Neanderthalers', *Journal of Archaeological Science*, 1975, 2, 161-3.

9. A.J. Steegman, 'Cold response body form and craniofacial shape in two racial groups of Hawaii', *American Journal of Physical Anthropology*, 1972,37, 193-222. S. Sergi, *The Neanderthal Palaeoanthropi in Italy*, 1958, reprinted in *Ideas on Human Evolution*, ed. W. Howells, Cambridge, Mass. 1962. C.S. Coon, *The Origin of Races*, London 1963. D.S. Brose and M.H. Wolpoff, 'Early Upper Palaeolithic man and late Middle Palaeolithic tools', *American Anthropologist*, 1971, 73, 1156-94.

10. Coon, 1963, op. cit.

11. C.B. Stringer, 'Population relationships of late Pleistocene hominids', *Journal of Archaeological Science*, 1974, 1, 317-42.

12. C.L. Brace, 'The fate of the "classic" Neanderthals', *Current Anthropology*, 1964, 5(1), 3-43. T.D. Stewart, 'The evolution of man in Asia as seen in the lower jaw', *Anthropology*, 1970, 263-6. H. Suzuki, 'The skull of the Amud man', in *The Amud Man and his Cave Site*, ed. H. Suzuki and F. Takai, Tokyo 1970.

13. M.M. Gerasimov, *The Face Finder*, trans. A.H. Brodrick, London 1971.

14. Brace, 1964, op. cit.

15. W.R. Farrand, 'Geological correlation of prehistoric sites in the Levant', *The Origin of Homo sapiens*, ed. F. Bordes, Unesco, Paris 1972. B. Vandermeersch, 'Récentes découvertes de squelettes humains à Qafza (Israel): essai d'interpretation', *The Origin of Homo sapiens*, ed. Bordes, pp. 49-54.

16. Brose and Wolpoff, 1971, op. cit.

17. A.M. Brues, 'Models of race and cline', *American Journal of Physical Anthropology*, 1972, 37, 389-400.

18. H.V. Vallois and B. Vandermeersch, 'Le crâne Moustérien de Qafzeh', *L'Anthropologie*, 1972, 76, 71-96.

19. G.M. Morant, 'Studies of Palaeolithic man II: a biometric study of neanderthaloid skulls and of their relationships to modern racial types', *Annals of Eugenics*, 1927, 2, 318-80. A. Hrdlička, *The Skeletal Remains of Early Man*, *Smithsonian Miscellaneous Collections*, New York 1930, 83, pp. 1-379. F.C. Howell, 'The evolutionary significance of variations and varieties of Neanderthal man', *Quarterly Review of Biology*, 1957, 32, 330-47. W.E. le Gros Clark, *The Fossil Evidence for Human Evolution*, Chicago 1966.

20. Suzuki, 1970, op. cit. J.L. Heim, 'L'encéphale néanderthalien de l'homme de la Ferrassie', *L'Anthropologie*, 1970, 74, 527-72.

21. G.R. De Beer, *Embryos and Ancestors*, Oxford 1950. M.F.A. Montague, 'Time, morphology and neoteny in the evolution of man', *American Anthropologist*, 1955, 47, 119-53. A.A. Abbie, 'The factor of timing in the emergence of distinctively human characteristics', *Proceedings of the Royal Society of Tasmania*, 1964, 98, 63-71. A.A. Abbie, 'A new approach to the problem of human evolution', *Transactions of the Royal Society of South Australia*, 1952, 75, 70-88. Stringer, 1974, op. cit. D. Collins, *The Human Revolution from Ape to Artist*, London 1976.

22. Brothwell, 1975, op. cit.

23. H. Ucko, *Endocrine Diagnosis*, London 1951.

24. H.V. Vallois, 'The social life of early man: the evidence of the skeleton', *Publications in Anthropology. Viking Fund* 1961, 31, 214-35.

25. E.S. Crelin, 'The Steinheim skull: a linguistic link', *Yale Scientific*, 1973, 48 (10). E.S. Crelin, 'Development of the upper respiratory system', *Chemical Symposia*, 1976, 28(3), 3-30.

26. P. Lieberman, 'Primate vocalizations and human linguistic ability', *Journal of the Acoustical Society of America*, 1968, 44, 1572-84. P. Lieberman, 'Towards a unified phonetic theory', *Linguistic Inquiry*, 1970, 1, 307-22.

27. J.C. Catford, *Fundamental Problems in Phonetics*, Edinburgh 1977.

28. P. Lieberman and E.S. Crelin, 'On the speech of Neanderthal man', *Linguistic Inquiry*, 1971, II(2).

29. W.G. Golding, *The Inheritors*, London 1955; a novel about the life and eventual extinction of the last group of Neanderthals alive on earth. Well worth reading.

30. D. Bolinger, *Aspects of Language*, 2nd ed., New York 1976.

31. F. Hoyle, *The Black Cloud*, London 1960; science fiction novel concerning the visit to earth of a superior intelligence.

32. J.H. Musgrave, 'How dextrous was Neanderthal man?', *Nature*, 1971, 233(5321), 538-41.

33. H.V. Vallois and H.L. Movius jnr., *Catalogue des Hommes Fossiles*, 1952, CR Cong. Geol. Intern, Algiers.

34. E.J. Trinkaus, 'Squatting among the Neanderthals: a problem in the behavioural interpretation of skeletal morphology', *Journal of Archaeological Science*, 1975, 327-51.

35. Vallois, 1961, op.cit.

36. E. Patte, *Les Néanderthaliens: Anatomie, Physiologie, Comparaisons*, Paris 1955.

37. Hrdlička, 1930, op. cit.

38. M. Boule and H.V. Vallois, 'Anthropologie', in *Les Grottes Paléolithiques des Beri-Sequal, Algérie*, ed. C. Arambourg, M. Boule, H.V. Vallois and R. Verneau, *Archives de L'Institut du Paléontologie Humaine*, 1934, mem.13. M. Boule and H.V. Vallois, *Fossil Men*, London 1957.

39. Oakley, Campbell, and Molleson, 1971, op. cit.

40. P.V. Tobias, 'Aspects of pathology and death among early hominids', *The Leech*, 1974, 44(3), 119-24. P.V. Tobias, *Man's Past and Future*, 5th Raymond Dart Lecture, Witwatersrand University Press, Johannesburg 1971.

41. Data from Vallois, 1961, op. cit.

42. C. Arambourg, 'Sur l'attitude, en station verticale, des Néanderthaliens', *Comptes Rendus des Séances de l'Academie des Sciences*, 1955, 240, 804-6, 1 fig. T. Dobzhansky, 'On species and races of living and fossil man', *American Journal of Physical Anthropology*, 1944, 2, 251-65, F.C. Howell, 'The place of Neanderthal man in human evolution', *American Journal of Physical Anthropology*, NS.9(4), 379-415. W. Howells, 'Neanderthal man: facts and figures', in *Palaeoanthropology: Morphology and Palaeoecology*, ed. R.H. Tuttle, The Hague 1975, pp.389-407.

3. Tools and Technology

1. F. Bordes, 'Essai de classification des industries Moustériennes', *Bulletin de la Société Préhistoire Française*, 1953, 50, 457-66. F. Bordes, 'Reflection on typology and technique in the Palaeolithic', *Arctic Anthropology*, 1969, 6, 1-29. P.A. Mellars, 'The Mousterian successors in south-west France', unpublished Ph.D. thesis, University of Cambridge, 1967. P.A. Mellars, 'The chronology of the Mousterian industries in the Périgord region', *Proceedings of the Prehistoric Society*, 1969, 35, 134-71.

2. F. Bordes, *A Tale of Two Caves*, New York 1972.

3. D. Peyrony, 'La Ferrassie', *Préhistoire*, 1934, 3, 1-92. M. Bourgon, 'Les industries Moustériennes et pre-Moustériennes du Périgord', *Archives de l'Institut de Paléontologie Humaine*, 1957, mem. 27. F. Bordes, 'Mousterian cultures in France', *Science*, 22 Sept. 1961.

4. Mellars, 1969, op.cit.

5. D. Collins and A. Collins, 'Excavations at Oldbury, Kent: new evidence for last glacial occupation in Britain', *Bulletin of the Institute of Archaeology, University of London*, 1970, 8-9, 151-76.

6. D. Roe, 'A study of handaxe groups of the British Lower and Middle Palaeolithic periods using methods of metrical and statistical analysis, with a gazetteer of British Lower and Middle Palaeolithic sites', unpublished Ph.D. thesis, University of Cambridge, 1967.

7. M.L. Shackley, 'The bout coupé handaxe as a cultural marker for the British Mousterian industries', in *Stone Tools as Cultural Markers*, pp.332-9, ed. R.V.S. Wright, Australian Institute of Aboriginal Studies, Canberra 1977.

8. Bordes, 1969, op.cit.

9. L.R. Binford and S.R. Binford, 'A preliminary analysis of functional variability in the Mousterian of Levallois facies', *American Anthropologist*, 1966, 68(2), 238-395.

10. H. Movius, 'The Mousterian cave of Teshik-Tash, south-eastern Uzbekistan, Central Asia', *American School of Prehistoric Research Bulletin*, 1953, XVII, 11-71.

11. M.L. Shackley, 'A contextual study of the Mousterian industry from Great Pan Farm, Isle of Wight', *Proceedings of the Isle of Wight Archaeological and Natural History Society*, 1973, 6(8), 542-54.

12. J. Constable, *The Neanderthals*, London 1973.

13. G. Ll. Isaac, 'Studies of early culture in East Africa', *World Archaeology*, 1970, 1, 1-28.

14. S.A. Semenov, *Prehistoric Technology*, translated by M.W. Thompson, London 1964.

15. L.H. Keeley, 'Technique and methodology in microwear studies: a critical review', *World Archaeology*, 1974, 5(3), 323-37. J. Nance, 'Functional interpretation from microscopic analysis', *American Antiquity*, 1971, 36, 361-6. G. Macdonald and D. Sanger, 'Some aspects of microscopic analysis and photomicrography: lithic artefacts', *American Antiquity*, 1968, 33, 237-40. M.L. Shackley, 'Stream abrasion of flint implements', *Nature*, 1974, 248, 501-2.

16. S. Kantman, 'Esquisse d'un procédé analytique pour l'étude macrographique des "enrochés"', *Quaternaria*, 1970, 13, 269-80. S. Kantman, 'Essai d'une méthode d'étude des "denticules" Moustériens pour discrimination des variables morpho-fonctionelles', *Quaternaria*, 1970, 13, 281-94. S. Kantman, '"Râclettes Moustériennes": une étude expérimental sur la distinction de rétouche intentionelle et les modifications du tranchant pour utilisation', *Quaternaria*, 1970, 13, 295-304.

17. S. Kantman, 'Essai sur le problème de rétouche d'utilisation dans l'étude du matériel lithique: premiers résultats', *Bulletin de la Société Préhistoire Française*, 1971, 68, 200-4.

18. R. Gould, D. Koster, and A. Sontz, 'A lithic assemblage of the Western Desert Aborigines of Australia', *American Antiquity*, 1971, 36, 149-69.

19. Ibid., p.166.

20. Binford and Binford, 1966, op.cit.

21. C. Girard, 'L'habitat et le mode de vie au paléolithique moyen à Arcy-sur-Cure (Yonne)', in *Les Structures d'Habitat au Paléolithique Moyen*, ed. L.F. Freeman, 1976, Colloque XI, IX Congres UISPP, Nice, pp. 49-63.

22. L. Freeman, 'Middle Palaeolithic dwelling remnants from Spain', in *Les Structures d'Habitat au Paléolithique Moyen*, ed. Freeman, pp. 36-48.

23. Except the pioneer studies of workers like: A.K. Behrensmayer, 'The taphonomy and palaeoecology of Plio-Pleistocene vertebrate assemblages east of Lake Rudolph, Kenya', *Bulletin of the Museum of Comparative Zoology*, 1975, 146(10), 473-578.

24. P. Biberson and E. Aguirre, 'Expériences de taille d'outils préhistoriques dans les os d'éléphant', *Quaternaria*, 1965, 7, 165-83.

25. M.H. Newcomer, 'Study and replication of bone tools from Ksar Akil', *World Archaeology*, 1974, 6(2), 138-54.

26. R.G. Klein, 'Early man on the eastern littoral of the Black Sea', *Ampurias*, 1969, 29, 1-23. R.G. Klein, *Ice-Age Hunters of the Ukraine*, Chicago 1973.

27. L. Vertes, *Tata, eine Multipaläolithische Travertin-Siedlungin Ungarn*, Budapest 1964.

28. K.P. Oakley, 'Use of fire by Neanderthal man and his precursors', in *Hundert Jahre Neanderthaler*, ed. G.H.R. von Koenigswald, Köln-Graz 1958, pp.267-70.

29. A. Leroi-Gourhan, 'La galerie Moustérienne de la Grotte du Renne (Arcy-sur-Cure, Yonne)', *Comptes Rendus de la Congrès Préhistorique Française*, Poitiers-Angoulême, 676-91.

30. R. Grahmann, *Urgeschichte der Menschheit*, 2nd ed., Stuttgart 1956.

31. A.C. Blanc, 'Torre in Petra, Saccopastore, Monte Circeo, on the position of the Mousterian in the Pleistocene sequence of the Rome area', in *Hundert Jahre Neanderthaler*, ed. von Koenigswald, pp.167-74.

32. C.S. Coon, *The Origin of Races*, London 1963.

4. Camps and Caves

1. G. Ll. Isaac, 'The diet of early man: aspects of archaeological evidence from Lower and Middle Pleistocene sites in Africa', *World Archaeology*, 1971, 2(3), 278-300.

2. G. Bosinski, 'Middle Palaeolithic structural remains from western central Europe', in *Les Structures d'Habitat au Paléolithique Moyen*, ed. L.F. Freeman, 1976, Colloque IV, IX Congrès USIPP, Nice, 64-77. G. Bosinski, 'Die mittel paläolithischen Funde im westlichen Mitteleuropa', *Fundamenta*, 1967, A/4, Köln-Graz. G. Bosinski, 'Arbeiten zur ältenen und mittleren Steinzeit in der Bundesrepublik Deutschland: 1949-74', *Ausgrabungen in Deutschland*, 1975, 1, 3-24. G. Bosinski *et al.*, 'Der paläolithische Fundplatz Rheindahlen, Ziegelei Dreesen-Westwand', *Bonner Jarbuch*, 1966, 166, 318-60. G. Bosinski and J. Kulick, 'Der mittelpaläolithische Fundplatz Buhlen, Kr. Waldeck, Vorbericht über die Grabungen 1966-69', *Germania*, 1973, 51, 1-41. D. Mania and V. Toepfer, *Königsame, Gleiderung, Okologie und Mittelpaläolithische Funde der Letzten Eiszeit*, 1973, Berlin.

3. G. Bohm-Blancke, *Altsteinzeitliche Rästplatze im Travertingebeit von Taubach, Weimar, Ehringsdorf*, 1960, Weimar: Alt-Thuringen IV.

4. Bosinski, 1967, op.cit.

5. Bosinski, 1976. op.cit.

6. Ibid.

7. C. Girard, 'L'habitat et le mode de vie au paléolithique moyen à Arcy-sur-Cure (Yonne)', in *Les Structures d'Habitat au Paléolithique Moyen*.

8. R.J. Klein, 'The middle Palaeolithic of the Crimea', *Arctic Anthropology*, 1965, 3(1), 34-68. I. Ivanova, *The Geological Age of Fossil Man*, Moscow 1965, pp.106-7. I. Ivanova, 'The geology of the Molodova multilevel Palaeolithic sites on the Middle Dnestr', *Anthropozoikum*, 1962, 11, 197-220 (in Russian).

9. A.P. Chernysh, 'The Lower and Middle Palaeolithic of the Dnestr region', *Trudy Komissii po Izucheniyu Chetvertichnovo Perioda*, 1965, 25 (in Russian).

10. F. Bordes, *A Tale of Two Caves*, New York 1972.
11. Ibid.
12. H. de Lumley, *Hortus Cave: The Neanderthal Hunters and their Environment*, Paris 1976.
13. L. Freeman, 'Middle Palaeolithic dwelling remnants from Spain', in *Les Structures d'Habitat au Paléolithique Moyen*. J. Gonzalez Echegaray and L. Freeman, *Cueva Morín: Excavationes 1966-8*, 1971, Patronato de las Cuevas Prehistóricas de la Provincia de Santander.

5. Hunting

1. J. Constable, *The Neanderthals*, London 1973.
2. J. Pfeiffer, *The Emergence of Man*, London 1970.
3. P. Mellars, 'The chronology of the Mousterian industries in the Perigord region', *Proceedings of the Prehistoric Society*, 1969, 35.
4. E. Bachler, *Das Alpine Paläolithikum der Schweiz*, Basel 1940. O. Abel and G. Kyrle, 'Die Drachenhöhle bei Mixnitz', *Spal. Monografien*, 1931, VII-VIII. M. Mottl, 'Die Repolusthöhle, eine Protoaurignacien-station bei Peggau in der Steirmark', *Verhandlungen der Geologischen Bundesamt*, 1949, 10-12. M. Mottl, 'Die Repolusthöhle bei Peggau und ihre eiszeitlichen Bewohner', *Archaeologica Austria*, 1950, 5. M. Mottl, 'Neue Grabungen in der Repolusthöhle bei Peggau in der Steirmark', *Mitteilungen des Museums fur Bergbau, Geologie und Technik am Landesmuseum Joanneum*, 1955, 15. V. Gabori-Csank, 'Le mode de vie et l'habitat au paléolithique moyen en Europe centrale', in *Les Structures d'Habitat au Paléolithique Moyen*, ed. L. Freeman, Colloque XI IV Congrès UISPP, Nice, 1976, pp.78-104. V. Gabori-Csank, *La Station du Páléolithique Moyen d'Erd, Hongrie*, Akademia Kiado, Budapest 1968. M. Gabori, 'The Palaeolithic of Hungary', *Les-Perigliatsial-Paleolit na Territorii*, 1969, Sredney i Vostochnoy Evropy, pp.252-67, (in Russian). M. Gabori, *Les Industries du Paléolithique Moyen entre les Alpes et l'Oural*, 1975, Budapest.
5. E. Schmid, *Höhlensforschung und Sedimentanalyse: ein Beitrag zur Datierung des Alpinen Paläolithikums*, Basel 1958. E. Schmid, 'Neue Grabung im Wilkirchli', *Ur-Schweitz*, 1961, 25.
6. H.G. Bandi, 'Zur Frage eine Banen – oder Opferkultes im ausgehended Altpaläolithikum der Alpinen Zone', *Helvetica Antiqua*, 1966. Gabori-Csank, 1976, op.cit.
7. Gabori-Csank, 1968, op.cit.
8. A.A. Milne, *Winnie-the-Pooh*, London 1926.
9. O. Kadic *et al.*, 'A cserépfalui Mussolini-barlang (Subalyuk)', *Geologica Hungarica. Series Paleontologica*, 1938, 14.
10. Gabori-Csank, 1976, op.cit.
11. R.G. Klein, *Ice Age Hunters of the Ukraine*, Chicago 1973. N.-K. Vereschagin, 'Primitive hunters and Pleistocene extinctions in the Soviet Union', in *Pleistocene Extinction*, ed. P.S. Martin and H.E. Wright, New Haven 1967, pp.365-98.
12. A.P. Chernysh, 'The Upper Palaeolithic of the middle Dnestr region', *Trudy Komissii po Izucheniyu Chetvertichnovo Perioda*, 1959, 15, 5-214, (in Russian).
13. I.G. Shovkopylas, *The Mezin Site*, Kiev 1965 (in Russian). A.N. Rogachev, 'Investigation of the remains of a primitive communal settlement of Upper

Palaeolithic time near the village of Ardeevo on the Seym in 1949', *Materialy i Issledovaniya po Arkheologii SSSR*, 1953, 39, 137-91 (in Russian).

14. K.M. Polikarpovich, *The Palaeolithic of the Upper Podneprov'e*, 1968, Akademiya Nauk., Belonus SSR, Minsk (in Russian). Klein, *Ice Age Hunters of the Ukraine*.

15. I.G. Pidoplichko, *Upper Palaeolithic Mammoth Cave Dwellings in the Ukraine*, Kiev 1969 (in Russian).

16. H.L. Movius, 'The Mousterian cave of Teshik-Tash, south-eastern Uzbekistan, C. Asia', *American School of Prehistoric Research Bulletin*, 1953, XVII, 11-71.

17. N.I. Popov, 'Concerning the tools of the Stone Age in northern and eastern Siberia', *Izvestiya Vostochno-Sibirskovo Otdela Russkovo Geograficheskovo Obshchestva*, 1878, 9, 1-12 (in Russian).

18. V.A. Gorodtsov, 'Results of investigation at the Palaeolithic site of Il'skaia', *Materialy i Issledovaniya po Arkheologii SSSR*, 1941, 2, 7-25 (in Russian).

19. J.B. Birdsell, 'Some predictions for the Pleistocene based on equilibrium systems among recent hunter-gatherers', in *Man the Hunter*, ed. R.E. Lee and I. DeVore, Chicago 1968, pp.229-49.

6. Ritual and Burial

1. P. Tailhard de Chardin, *The Phenomenon of Man*, London 1959.

2. P.V. Tobias, *Man's Past and Future*, Johannesburg 1971.

3. D. Peyrony, 'La Ferrassie', *Préhistoire*, 1934, 3, 1-92.

4. H.V. Vallois, 'La découverte du squelette du Moustier', *L'Anthropologie*, 1939, XLIX, 776-8.

5. Peyrony, 1934, op.cit.

6. L. Bardon and J. and A. Bouyssonie, 'Découverte d'un squelette humain Moustérien à la Chapelle-aux-Saints (Corrèze)', *Comptes Rendus Hebdomadaires des Séances de l'Academie des Sciences*, Paris 1908, 147, 1414-5.

7. C.S. Coon, *The Origin of Races*, London 1963. A.J. Jelinek, 'Neanderthal man and *Homo sapiens* in central and eastern Europe', *Current Anthropology*, 1969, X(5), 475-503. K.P. Oakley, *Framework for Dating Fossil Man*, London 1969. R.S. Solecki, *Shanidar: The Humanity of Neanderthal Man*, London 1971.

8. G.A. Bonch-Osmalovskii, 'Résultats de l'étude du paléolithique de Crimée, transactions II', *Congrès de l'Association du Quaternaire*, 1935, 5, 113-78. J. Fraipont and M. Lohest, 'La race humaine de Néanderthal ou de Canstadt en Belgique: récherches ethnographiques sur les ossements humains découverts dans les dépôts quaternaires d'une grotte à Spy et détermination de leur âge géologique', *Annales de Biologie*, 1887, band VII, 587-757.

9. A.A. Formosov, 'New data on the palaeolithic person from Starosel'e', *Sovietskaia Etnografia*, 1957, 2, 124-30 (in Russian).

10. A. Roginski, 'Morphological features of the skull of the child from the late Mousterian level of the cave of Starosel'e', *Sovietskaia Etnografia*, 1954, 1, 27-41 (in Russian). Formosov, in *Sovietskaia Etnografia*, 1957, 2.

11. R.G. Klein, 'The Middle Palaeolithic of the Crimea', *Arctic Anthropology*, 1965, 3(1).

12. M. Gerasimov, *People of the Stone Age*, Moscow 1964 (in Russian).

13. V.I. Gromov, 'The palaeontological and archaeological basis of the

stratigraphy of the continental deposit of the Quaternary period in the USSR', *Trudy Institut Geologicheskikh Nauk*, 1948, Akademia Nauk. SSR, Vyp.64, Geologicheskaya Seriya 17 (in Russian).

14. Solecki, 1971, op.cit.

15. F.H. Bordes, ed., *The Origin of Homo sapiens*, Unesco, Paris 1972. F.H. Bordes, 'La question périgordienne', in *La Préhistoire: Problèmes et Tendances*, C.N.R.S. Paris 1968, pp.59-70.

16. T.D. Stewart, 'First views of the restored Shanidar I skull', *Sumer*, 1958, XIV, 1-2, 90-8. T.D. Stewart, 'Restoration and study of the Shanidar I Neanderthal skeleton in Baghdad, Iraq', *Year Book of the American Philosophical Society*, 1958, 274-8. T.D. Stewart, 'Form of the pubic bone in Neanderthal man', *Science*, 1960, CXXXI (3411), 1437-8. T.D. Stewart, 'The skull of Shanidar II', *Sumer*, 1961, XVII, 1-2, 97-106. T.D. Stewart, 'Neanderthal scapulae with special attention to the Shanidar Neanderthal from Iraq', *Anthropos*, 1962, LVII, 3-6, 778-800. T.D. Stewart, 'Shanidar skeletons IV and VI, *Sumer*, 1963, XIX, 1-2, 8-26.

17. A. Leroi-Gourhan, 'Le Néanderthalien IV de Shanidar', *Bulletin de la Société Préhistorique Française, Comptes Rendus des Séances Mensuelles*, 1963, XLV(3), 79-83.

18. C.S. Coon, *The Living Races of Man*, London 1966.

19. S.R. Binford, 'A structural comparison of disposal of the dead in the Mousterian and Upper Palaeolithic', *Southwestern Journal of Anthropology*, 1968, XXIV(2), 139-54.

20. H. Martin, 'Sur un squelette humain de l'époque Moustérienne trouvé en Charente, *Comptes Rendus de l'Academie des Sciences*, 1911, 153, 728-30.

21. H. Martin, 'Sur la répartition des ossements humains dans le gisement de la Quina (Charente)', *L'Anthropologie*, 1921, 31, 340-2.

22. H. Virchow, 'Sur le Moustier', *L'Anthropologie*, 1940, 49, 776-8.

23. H. Klaatsch and O. Hauser, 'Homo aurignaciensis hausensis', *Praehistorische Zeitschrift*, 1910, 1, 173-338.

24. D. de Sonneville-Bordes, 'Position stratigraphique et chronologie relative des restes remains du Paléolithique supérieur entre Loire et Pyrénées', *Annales de Paléontologie*, 1959, 45, 19-51.

25. Dates from S. Binford, 1968, op.cit.

26. Ibid.

27. F.C. Howell, 'Upper Pleistocene stratigraphy and early man in the Levant', *Proceedings of the American Philosophical Society*, 1959, 103, 1-65. F.C. Howell, 'Upper Pleistocene men of the south-west Asian Mousterian', in *Hundert Jahre Neanderthaler*, ed. G.H.R. von Koenigswald, Köln-Graz 1958, pp.185-98.

28. S.R. Binford, 'Variability and change in the near eastern Mousterian of Levallois facies', in *New Perspectives in Archaeology*, ed. S.R. and L.R. Binford, Chicago 1968. S.R. Binford, 'Early Upper Pleistocene adaptations in the Levant', *American Anthropologist*, 1968, 70(4), 707-17.

29. A.P. Okladnikov, *Paléolithique et Néolithique de l'USSR*, 1956, Annales du Centre d'Etude et de Documentation Paléontologique, Paris (French translation).

30. H. Movius, 'The Mousterian cave of Teshik-Tash, S.E. Uzbekistan, C. Asia', *American School of Prehistoric Research Bulletin*, 1953, XVII, 11-71.

31. K. Gorjanovic-Kramberger, 'Über ein vermütliches Feuerholz des Homo primigenius aus Krapina', *Verhandlungen der Gesellschaft Deutscher Naturforscher und Artze*, 1919, 81, Teil 2, 211-13. S. Vukovic, 'On the dating of the Krapina man finds', *Current Anthropology*, 1969, 10(1), 126.

32. J. Constable, *The Neanderthals*, London 1973.

33. A.R. Blanc, 'Some evidence for the ideologies of early man', in *Social Life of Early Man*, ed. S.L. Washburn, Chicago 1961.

34. Tobias, 1971, op.cit.

35. A.C. Blanc, 'L'homme fossile de Monte Circeo', *L'Anthropologie*, 1939, 44, 253-64. A.C. Blanc, 'Avifauna artica, crioturbazioni e testimonianze di soliflussi nel Pleistocene medio-superiore di Roma e di Torre in Petra: il periodo glaciale Nomentano nel quadro della serie di glaciazioni riconosciute nel Lazio', *Quarternaria*, 1955, 2, 187-200. A.C. Blanc, 'Torre in Petra, Saccopastore, Monte Circeo, on the position of the Mousterian in the Pleistocene sequence of the Rome area', in *Hundert Jahre Neanderthaler*, ed. von Koenigswald.

36. Constable, 1973, op.cit.

37. M.L. Shackley, *Rocks and Man*, London 1977.

38. A.C. Blanc, 'A new palaeolithic cultural element probably of ideological significance: the clay pellets of the cave of the Basua (Savona)', *Quaternaria*, 1957, 4.

39. J. Pfeiffer, *The Emergence of Man*, London 1970.

40. A.C. Blanc, 'The oldest human footprints?', *Illustrated London News*, 1 March 1955, 377-9.

41. P. de Mortillet, *Origine de Culte des Morts: Les Sépultures Préhistoriques*, 1914, Gamber, Paris. H.V. Vallois, 'La durée de la vie chez l'homme de Néanderthal', in *Hundert Jahre Neanderthaler*, ed. von Koenigswald. F.M. Bergounioux, 'Spiritualité de l'homme de Néanderthal', in *Hundert Jahre Neanderthaler*, ed. von Koenigswald.

7. Survival or Extinction

1. C.L. Brace, 'The fate of the 'classic' Neanderthal: a consideration of hominid catastrophism', *Current Anthropology*, 1964, 5, 3-43.

2. F. Bordes, *The Origin of Homo sapiens*, 1972, Proceedings of the Paris Symposium, Unesco, Paris, September 1969.

3. F.E. Zeuner, 'The replacement of Neanderthal man by *Homo sapiens*', in *Hundert Jahre Neanderthaler*, ed. G.H.R. von Koenigswald, Köln-Graz 1958, 312-17.

4. C.L. Brace, 'Cultural factors in the evolution of human dentition', in *Culture and the Evolution of Men*, ed. M.F.A. Montague, 1962, Oxford University Press, New York.

5. D.R. Pilbeam, 'Man's earliest ancestors', *Science Journal*, February 1967.

6. F.C. Howell, 'Pleistocene glacial ecology and the evolution of classic Neanderthal man', *Southwestern Journal of Anthropology*, 1952, 8 (4), 377-410.

7. C.S. Coon, *The Origin of Races*, London 1963.

8. J. Pfeiffer, *The Emergence of Man*, London 1970.

9. A. Keith and T.D. McCowen, 'Mount Carmel man: his bearing on the ancestry of modern races', in *Early Man*, ed. G.G. MacCurdy, Philadelphia 1937, pp. 41-52.

10. T.D. MacCowen and A. Keith, *The Stone Age of Mount Carmel*, vol.2, *The Fossil Human Remains from the Levalloiso-Mousterian*, Oxford 1939. B. Vandermeersch, 'Les nouveaux squelettes Moustériens découverts a Qafzeh (Israel) et leur signification', *Comptes Rendus de l'Academie des Sciences*, Paris 1969, 268, 2562-5. A. Thoma, 'Métissage ou transformation? Essai sur les hommes fossiles de Palestine', *L'Anthropologie*, 1957-8, 60, 519-34. A. Ronen, *Tirat-Carmel, A Mousterian Open Air Site in Israel*, memoir 3, Institute of Archaeology, Tel-Aviv University. A.E. Garrod and D.M.A. Bate, *The Stone Age of Mount Carmel*, vol.1, Oxford 1937. D.R. Brothwell, 'The people of Mount Carmel', *Proceedings of the Prehistoric Society*, 1961, 27, 155-9. S.R. Binford, 'Late Middle Palaeolithic adaptations in the Levant and their possible consequences', *Bioscience*,

1970, 20, 280-3. M.F. Ashley-Montagu, 'Review of *The Stone Age at Mount Carmel*', *American Anthropologist*, 1940, 42, 518-22.

11. T.D. Stewart, 'The problems of the earliest claimed representative of *Homo sapiens*', *Cold Spring Harbour Symposium on Quantitative Biology*, 1951, 15, 97-107.

12. A. Ronen, 'The Skuhl burials: an archaeological review', in *Les Sépultures Néanderthaliennes*, ed. B. Vandermeersch, 1976, Colloque XII, IX Congrès UISPP, Nice.

13. A.J. Jelinek *et al.*, 'New excavations at the Tabun cave, Mount Carmel, Israel, 1967-72: a preliminary report', *Paléorient*, 1973, 1, 151-83.

14. Data from Ronen, 1976, op.cit.

15. H. Suzuki and F. Takai, *The Amud Man and his Cave Site*, Tokyo 1970. R.E.F. Leakey, K.W. Butzer and M. Day, 'Early *Homo sapiens* remains from the Omo river region of south-west Ethiopia', *Nature*, 1969, 222, 1132-8.

16. Ibid.

17. H. Suzuki *et al.*, *Studies on the Graves, Coffin Contents, and Skeletal Remains of the Togugawa Shoguns and their Families at the Zojoji Temple*, Tokyo 1967 (English abstract).

18. D. Ferembach, 'L'ancêtre de l'homme du paléolithique supérieur était – il néanderthalien?', in *The Origin of Homo sapiens*, ed. Bordes.

19. L. Pradel, 'Transition from Mousterian to Perigordian: skeletal and industrial', *Current Anthropology*, February, 1966.

20. F. Bordes, 'Le paléolithique supérieur et moyen de Jabrud (Syrie) et la question du Pre-Aurignacien', *L'Anthropologie*, 1955, 59, 486-507. E. Ennouchi, 'Un néanderthalien: l'homme du Jebel Ighoud (Maroc)', *L'Anthropologie*, 1962, 66, 279-99. B. Vandermeersch, 'Position stratigraphique et chronologie rélative des restes humains du paléolithique moyen dans le Sud-Ouest de la France', *Annales de Paléontologie Vertébrés*, 1965, 51, 109-10. T.F. Lynch, 'The "lower Perigordian" in French archaeology', *Proceedings of the Prehistoric Society*, 1966, 32, 156-98. A.D. Lacaille, 'Châtelperron: a new survey of its palaeolithic industry', *Archaeologia*, 1947, 92.

21. F. Bordes, 'Essai de classification des industries Moustériennes', *Bulletin de la Société Préhistoire Française*, 1953, 50, 457-66.

Index

Abbie, A.A., 136
Abel, O., 140
Acheulean, 8; fire, 52; French, 56; hunting, 70
Africa: evolution in, 9; site classification, 54-5
Aguirre, E., 139
Almas, 129-33
Alpine sites: industries, 45, 73; hunting, 73-5, 78-9
Ambrona, 6, 10; bone tools, 51, 68
Amud, 20, 21, 123-4
Arago, 10
Arambourg, C., 137
Arcy-sur-Cure, 10; fire, 52; bone tools, 50; structures, 57, 126-7
Ardeevo, 58, 81
art objects, 51-8
arthritis: at La Chapelle, 3, 18; at Krapina, 30; at Shanidar, 30, 94; in gibbons, 30
Asinus hydruntinus, 78
Ashley-Montague, M.F., 144
Australia: early man, 12
Australopithecus: appearance, 19; brain capacity, 24-5; evolution, 9; 'osteodontokeratic' industry, 50

Bachler, E., 140
Badl-Höhle, 73
Bandi, H.G., 73, 140
Bardon, L. 85, 141
Bate, A.E., 143
bear hunting: Alpine sites, 72-3, 78; Erd, 76-8

Behrensmayer, A.K., 138
Bergouniuux, F.M., 135, 143
Betula nana, 58
Biberson, P., 139
'Bigfoot', 128-33
Binford, L., 46, 138, 142
Binford, S.R., 98, 102, 138, 142, 143
Birdsell, J.B., 141
Blanc., A.C., 53, 109, 139, 142, 143
Bohm-Blancke, G., 135, 139
bolas, 69, 71
Bolinger, D., 137
Bonch-Osmalovskii, G.H., 89, 141
bone: cooking, 53; fuel, 53, 80; marrow, 53, 80; utilisation, 49-51
Bonifay, E., 63
Bordes, F., 35-40, 44-5, 135, 136, 137, 138, 140, 142, 143, 144
Bosinski, G., 139
Boule, M., 16-17, 117, 135, 137
Bourgon, M., 137
bout coupé handaxes, 40-5
Bouyssonie, J. and A., 85, 141
Bowler, J.M., 135
Brace, C.L., 117, 119, 135, 136, 143
Braidwood, R.J., 135
brain capacity, 24-5
brain eating, 107-9
Breitinger, E., 135
Brose, D.S., 135, 136
Brothwell, D., 22-3, 118, 136, 143
Brues, A.M., 136
Butzer, K.W., 135, 144

Campbell, B.G., 135, 137